FOXWA

C000151302

Martin He

Foreword by
Stephen Harris

Whittet Books

First published 1997
© 1997 by Martin Hemmington
Whittet Books Ltd, 18 Anley Road, London W14 0BY
Illustrations © 1997 by David Hall
Reprinted 1999
All rights reserved. No part of this publication may be reproduced, transmitted or
stored in a retrieval system, in any form or by any means, without permission in
writing from Whittet Books Limited.

The right of Martin Hemmington to be identified as the author of this work
has been asserted in accordance with the Copyright, Designs and Patents Act 1988.

British Library Cataloguing in Publication Data. A catalogue record for this book is
available from the British Library.

ISBN 1 873580 31 2
The author and publisher are grateful to the following for permission to reproduce
photographs (all other photographs are by the author): Adam Chennells (pp. 27
and 77); Steve Magennis (p. 9); Diane Wilson (pp. 17, 58, 65)

Acknowledgments

I would like to thank Dorothy Mann for tirelessly working through my first draft of
this book and for correcting many of the spelling mistakes and grammatical errors.
I would also like to express my thanks to David Hall for supplying the excellent
illustrations throughout the book, and to Adam Chennells, Diane Wilson and
Steve Magennis for giving me the permission to use some of their photographs.
My special thanks to Professor Stephen Harris, a world renowned expert on foxes,
for his useful suggestions and for doing the Foreword.
Last, but by no means least, a very big thank you to both Robert and Elizabeth,
the co-ordinators of C.A.R.E.S. Wildlife Hospital in Cambridge, for taking in
many of the injured and sick foxes we have been out to rescue over the years; two
people whose constant dedication and commitment to wildlife always proves
inspirational.
Finally, to Vivienne, for whom I dedicate this book, for without her none of
this would have been possible. She has, over the years, watched my interest in foxes
grow into an obsession and she has supported me morally and financially every step
of the way. Vivienne actively encouraged me to write this book and gave me many
useful suggestions and honest opinions throughout its progress, never once doubt-
ing that it would, one day, be published.

Printed and bound in the UK by WBC

Contents

Foreword

As a young teenager living on the Essex side of London in the early 1960s, my opportunities to watch wildlife were somewhat limited, and my days were spent studying amphibians, insects and birds. But their fascination rapidly palled the day I saw my first fox. Admittedly it was just a brief glimpse as it darted across the road, and had it not been under a street light, I could easily have dismissed it as a cat. Yet whilst I was sure it was a fox, I still found it hard to believe. Were there really foxes in such a heavily urbanised area? I went to the library, but there were no books on foxes, other than those extolling the virtues of fox hunting. So I contacted the local natural history society to try to learn more, but to no avail: no one appeared to know that there were foxes in my part of London, and my own observation was dismissed as a mistake.

With time, however, I slowly collected more evidence to show that there really was a local fox population, and that it appeared to be growing. Scent marks on gates, faeces left on waste ground, calls in the night, and sightings of a fox darting across the road, all became more frequent. And eventually I found the body of a fox killed by a passing car, my first specimen to examine for fleas, to dissect, and to prepare the skull and skeleton, all done in my mother's kitchen. I was lucky enough to be witnessing the foxes colonising my part of London.

It soon became apparent that foxes were already present in large numbers on the south and west sides of London, as so clearly shown by Bunny Teagle's fascinating survey published by the London Natural History Society in 1967. Yet whilst the capital's foxes were well and truly on the map, people were still unsure whether foxes were established in other cities, or if the odd sightings were escapees or occasional itinerants exploring the urban area. So Elaine Hurrell organised the first fox rally in Plymouth, where people drove round the city at night recording fox sightings. This was soon followed by similar rallies in Bristol and several towns in Essex. And, yes, all saw large numbers of foxes. The urban fox phenomenon had arrived.

Whilst it was easy to document the distribution of urban foxes, actually studying foxes, whether they were living in our towns or in the countryside, was a lot more difficult. In 1948 Ernest Neal published his New Naturalist Monograph on *The Badger*. This was the first detailed field study on badgers and proved to be a landmark, stimulating generations of enthusiastic badger watchers. But badgers are easy to study: their behaviour is predictable, they leave obvious field signs, and they are easy to approach and watch. None of this is true for foxes; except when they have cubs, foxes use earths infrequently, are seen only fleetingly, and are virtually impossible to observe. It is hardly surprising therefore that the first detailed field study on foxes was not published until 1968, twenty years after that on badgers. In his book *Wild Fox*, Roger Burrows described the results of his three-year study of the foxes in a small area of Gloucestershire. Roger had started his study at the same time that I was undertaking my first forays into the world of foxes, and we had both experienced the same frustrations: there was a complete lack of useful information on even the most basic aspects of fox behaviour. So to me his book was as important as Ernest Neal's on badgers: it stimulated me to learn more about foxes for myself. Once started, foxes became an obsession and rapidly dominated my life, something I have never regretted.

So much has changed since I started my early fox studies. Then even friends in the Essex Mammal Group could not understand why I was so fascinated by an animal they considered to be smelly, sly and verminous. Yet in the intervening period a succession of television documentaries and a plethora of books about both rural and urban foxes has led to a dramatic change in attitudes to foxes The idea that foxes are 'vermin' or 'pests' that need to be controlled whenever and however possible has been replaced by the realisation that foxes should be valued. One in ten households in Bristol regularly feeds the foxes in their gardens, and more and more farmers and landowners are coming to appreciate foxes for their role in controlling rabbits. The vast majority of the public, both rural and urban dwellers, are now opposed to fox hunting.

As part of these changing attitudes to foxes, since 1993 we have had a National Fox Welfare Society, thanks to Martin Hemmington. This has played a major role in furthering the appreciation and understanding of foxes and, following Martin's lead, local fox groups are springing up around the country. Yet despite this ever-increasing fascination with anything vulpine, someone who wants to study foxes for themselves will face many of the problems I first encountered thirty years ago: it is still very difficult to know how to start because there is no ready source of practical advice and helpful hints on field craft. Martin's book is the first to fill this essential gap in the fox literature, and I hope it stimulates a new generation of keen fox watchers to study this most fascinating, but frustratingly elusive, member of our fauna.

Stephen Harris
Professor of Environmental Sciences
University of Bristol

Introduction

Why foxes ?

After ruling out the wolf to watch and study in this country – since there were none – I decided to turn my attentions to the only wild dog remaining in this country: a wild dog that even today captures the imagination of children and adults alike. It survives in a diversity of habitats; it epitomises the word 'adaptability'. It is this amazing adaptability, coupled with its non-selective eating habits that has led to its ultimate success. It not only survives next to man, but thrives: it is of course the red fox.

'Cunning' and 'sly' are just two of the characteristics attributed to the fox, although I suppose if one were a fox then this would be a compliment, for both words imply intelligence. Is the fox really this crafty animal, who appears to reap its revenge on man by taking his livestock? Is the fox really the bloodthirsty animal that we are all taught about on the parental knee? Is the fox really Public Enemy Number One?

Unfortunately, despite all we read about the fox's importance in the finely balanced scales of nature, the legends and fables of yester-year still persist, legends and fables that feed on our ignorance and do the fox a grave injustice. If the lion is the king of the jungle, why then is not the fox the king of our countryside ?

With many questions inside my head, I took to the fields in search of answers but, after many fruitless journeys, I decided to read as much on the fox as I could. Unfortunately the information I sought was missing; although all the books offered the reader a wealth of information on fox biology, sociology, radio-tracking, ear-tagging, etc, they all missed the basics – how to find, attract and watch foxes, the missing link that I needed so desperately. (Hence this book.)

I was blind to the signs and deaf to the sounds. Despite this I still journeyed across fields and meadows in all weathers and at all times searching, yet not really knowing what for. Even with more information I still failed to find my fox family to watch and study. It was so frustrating. I can only liken it to estimating a time for a journey, yet not knowing where to start out from. Then, as if the vulpine god of fox watchers had heard my prayers, after six months of observing nothing, luck, not judgement, turned in my favour.

It was about 8.30 in the evening, when I decided to take my dog for a walk and, as I reached the barred gate from which I had always started and finished my fox walks, I noticed a fox strolling up the field, oblivious to our presence. Once this fox had foraged its way halfway up the field, I observed another one coming from the other side of the field, and then another, closely followed by four cubs. My heart raced with excitement, and in my ignorance I attempted to observe differences in the foxes so as to name them.

The fox that had travelled the closest I named 'Two-Tone' due to the two-tone appearance of the coat. It was some time later that I realised the two-tone appearance was shared by most of the adult members. They were all going through the summer moult!

In my first few months of watching, I made many other mistakes: through inexperience I would allow myself to be detected by the fox; I would wear the wrong clothes and choose the wrong places to leave food and watch.

Looking back, the biggest mistake of all was the inaccuracy of my observations; things I would note down were not those I had observed, they were things I thought could have been happening. In hindsight there is a big difference. Despite such a catalogue of mistakes, from that warm June evening onwards I became hooked. On my visits to the area, I began to notice fox signs; it was as if they had newly been placed there, but in fact it was just that I had passed them by before. Field signs left behind by the fox became so obvious. Of course nobody had just put them there; now I was beginning to look in the right places.

Learning some of the many instincts and behaviours of the fox's prey is worth doing. Rabbits when danger is approaching will stamp their hind feet, or stand on their back legs for a better look. Warning calls from roosting birds betray the presence of foxes, calls that until then I had failed to hear. My eyes and ears were opening to the sights and sounds of nature. My foxwatching apprenticeship was just beginning.

You of course will make your own mistakes, you will come to your own conclusions, but this is all part of the fun. By outlining my mistakes, I do not think for one minute you will cease to make any. But by telling you of my observations, some of the things I have done that proved successful, I just hope to be able at least to provide some of the missing links, so you may avoid the fruitless hours of unrewarded patience I endured.

The red fox can be found in a diversity of habitats around the world. Information on the various habitats and the foxes that inhabit them could easily fill this book, so to could my views on fox-hunting and fox destruction, yet this material would not help you in your search for a fox family to watch and study. I have attempted to keep the information within this book as simple as possible as well as being comprehensive. This is also true of the chapter on research; what would be the use of a chapter devoted to ear-tagging or radio-tracking if it is out of the reach of the ordinary fox watcher?

In most of the books you read, the author offers his or her views on certain observations they have made. This book will be no exception. My views and observations may conflict with those in other books you may have read on foxes; I leave you to make your own conclusions.

My ultimate aim in writing this book is to help the foxes, foxes that have been persecuted for centuries through ignorance or people's refusal to believe the facts. I do not expect anyone to become passionate about foxes and want to do something positive for their welfare if they have never had the opportunity to watch one in the wild. If through this book people go out and watch foxes and their opinions of the fox

The secretive red fox at last climbed the ladder of popularity.

change, if a greater understanding of the fox can be achieved, then I will be satisfied.

Foxwatching is without a doubt an art, and attempting to be one step ahead of the fox is an art in itself. Yet, armed with a little understanding of the fox, and the signs it leaves behind, you too can get an insight into its secretive dark world and ultimately share the nights in the shadow of the fox.

—1—
The Fox

There are twenty-one species of fox around the world, but I will talk about only one, as it is only one that you are likely to observe wild in this country – the red fox. The Latin name for it is *Vulpes vulpes*. The word 'vulpine' describes fox behaviour. The female fox is called a 'vixen' and the male fox a 'dog'; their offspring or litter are called 'cubs'. The dog fox is usually slightly heavier, by around two pounds, and larger by a centimetre or so, than the vixen. Attempting to observe the difference through size alone in the field is almost impossible. A clue is that the dog fox will cock its leg when urinating whilst the vixen will squat.

Although the general term for *Vulpes vulpes* is the red fox, many colour variations exist, red being predominant. The coat can be better described as more of an orange brown. Black-and-white foxes very rarely occur in this country but both have been recorded. Most pictures show the fox having a large white tip to its tail. Whilst this is common, it is not the invariable rule and it certainly does not mean the fox with the white-tipped tail is the male. Both sexes can and do have white tips. Some however do not have any, while others can have black tips to theirs; nothing is uniform.

Foxes breed only once a year; a built-in control mechanism ensures they do not over-breed: the male can mate only from November to February, and the vixen will be on heat for only three days during this season. After much ritualized courtship the pair mate.

Family units

Although some foxes, called 'itinerant foxes', do not hold a territory, most have one that they will defend. It has been said that foxes defend a territory to ensure a regular food supply, or else to secure a mate. I feel this is a little like, what came first – the chicken or the egg? That is to say if a dog fox takes a territory to ensure he has a vixen to mate, then presumably the vixen must have been tempted into the defended territory knowing that it would provide her and any litters with a relatively safe environment and a regular supply of food. So each is as important as the other. What would be the use of a defended territory with no regular food supply, nor a vixen with which to mate?

Most fox territories will be large enough to guarantee a regular supply of food throughout the year for the family of foxes. They will contain areas of good worming pastures (foxes are fond of eating worms), of orchards for fruit and meadows for voles. It may be that in most months of the year there is more than enough food for the pair of foxes, and because the territory is fairly large it would take a lot of defending. Hence in some fox families you can have up to eight adult members, whilst in others only the breeding pair.

However many foxes there are in the family group, usually only the dominant pair will mate and produce cubs. Other adult members of the family still have a role to play in fox society. Let us assume, for example, a dog fox and vixen have just found a vacant territory and mated. Let us further assume our pair of foxes have produced five cubs, which is average; what usually happens is that the cubs when adult will disperse from their natal area in an attempt to attract a mate and find a territory of their own. If the family's territory could easily contain and feed three more adult foxes and there is room to stay in this area, then some of the cubs may choose to do just that, with the guarantee of a regular food supply. Although the male cubs sometimes do stay in their natal area it is usually the female cubs that will stay on.

So, now we have the breeding pair, plus, say, three sub-adult vixens within the territory. There are now five foxes that can defend the territory, but what happens when the mating season comes around again? Usually only the dominant pair will mate. To ensure that all the vixens within the territory do not also produce a litter of cubs, the dominant vixen will suppress the other vixens from mating, by generally pushing them around, therefore only she produces a litter. This litter is guaranteed the best chance because it is the only one produced and there is no competition for food.

Although suppressed from mating, the three daughters of the vixen will still carry food to her and her cubs. They will act as aunties to the cubs in that they will babysit for them, take them out hunting and play with them. The vixens that have stayed on within the territory are guaranteed a regular food supply. The one thing they have given up is their right to breed.

So if they cannot breed, ensuring that the litter of cubs their mother has had survives and thrives ensures that at least some of their own genes (i.e. their common mother's) will survive through other generations. Some vixens will go on to displace their mother or at the very least replace her when she dies, another good reason for the subordinate vixens to stay at home.

What with defending territories, and suppressing other vixens, one could easily assume that the foxes are forever fighting. Although fights do occur, they are not as regular as one might expect.

Like a domestic dog out on his walk, cocking his leg up at every available signpost, the dog fox will patrol the borders of his territory leaving calling cards by way of urination and defecation. These serve as reminders to would-be trespassing foxes that the area is occupied and defended. In addition the foxes will use a number of different vocal calls, some to stay in contact with members of the family, others to warn trespassing foxes away. If a trespassing fox chooses to ignore the warnings, a fight will take place, sometimes even to the death.

Within the family, domination of the subordinates very rarely results in bloodshed. When observed it can only be described as bullying. The dominant fox approaches the subordinate, tail held high, ears erect, walking stiffly. The subordinate either chooses to run, in which case she may be chased for a short distance, or adopts a submissive posture. The submissive posture is the opposite of the dominant posture: rather than looking big, the submissive fox will attempt to look as small as possible; rather than ears being erect, the submissive fox will have them flat against its head, and its tail will be between its back legs rather than held high (see illustration p. 68, submissive posture). This submissive posture will usually be enough to guarantee an all-out attack is avoided. If this fails the submissive fox will possibly roll on its back, screeching, the signal meaning to the dominant fox complete surrender. Most interactions between a dominant fox and a submissive one will be settled without any contact. Each fox however needs a place within the family structure. There will always be a top fox and a bottom fox: sorting out these differences usually does not result in bloodshed or death.

If two of the non-breeding vixens meet, both possibly feel superior, but neither is confident; a mixture of aggression and submission will be observed. Lots of pushing and body slamming will take place, lots of clicking noises coming from both. If this fails to settle their differences they will both go up on the hind legs, their forepaws resting on each other's shoulders (see illustration p. 72 fox trot). With mouths agape they will scream at each other. The victor is the one who manages to push the other one off balance, much like a slim version of Sumo wrestling. The victor will chase the other fox away; the loser will flee, sometimes screaming. In what can only be described as the fox trot, their differences are settled with one party's pride hurt, but nothing worse.

Despite such conflicts, foxes are sociable animals: they often meet whilst out foraging; they groom one another, although usually it is the dominant foxes that receive the most attention. They play with one another, adopting a play stance, much like what you can observe in a domestic dog, and they initiate games of chase. It is not always dominance versus submission.

Within a family unit, sometimes there may be multiple litters. The two mothers may den together; at other times the dominant vixen will kill the other litter of cubs. The reason for this breakdown in the rules of fox society could be that there has been a breakdown in family cohesion: perhaps a dominant vixen has been killed, therefore leaving submissive vixens free to mate. Whatever the reason, it is clear that any sort of control on the numbers of foxes, be it fox-hunting, snaring or shooting, will have no significant effect on the number of foxes and can sometimes lead to multiple litters being produced. The best way of controlling the number of foxes is apparent: leave them alone.

Fox cubs

It has been said that once a dog fox has mated with a vixen, he plays no part in the rearing of the cubs. Although this may be true on some occasions where a dog fox has mated with two vixens from different areas, the dog fox does often help, not only in providing for the cubs but also for the vixen when she is kennelled down before and after giving birth. (She will become inactive for the final days of her pregnancy and rely on the dog fox.) After a gestation of 53 days, the vixen gives birth to her cubs: usually in March, the average litter size being four or five. The dog fox will have supplied the vixen with food at the mouth of the earth during her denning period and will continue to do so.

The cubs when born are blind and deaf and remain so for the first 11 or so days; they weigh approximately 100gm (3½oz) and, because they are unable to regulate their own body heat, they rely solely on the vixen for both food and warmth. In turn the vixen relies on her dog fox to provide her meals. Due to the cubs' reliance on the vixen, she will in the first couple of weeks very rarely leave their side. There are exceptions, however, and one of these occurred in the area where I study foxes. The dominant dog fox was killed on the road in March, a very critical period for the vixen. The vixen was then forced to come out looking for food herself, which meant leaving her cubs alone. The food I supplied no doubt helped her in her time of need, and once she had crammed her mouth full of the offerings she would retreat to the earth.

The vixen managed successfully to rear her three healthy looking cubs. What intrigued me was not so much the vixen's dedication to her cubs, but in the vixen's time of need, where were the aunties? Through many hours of research I was able to determine that including the dog fox and vixen there were at least another six family members. Could it be that the aunties play an active part in looking after the cubs only when they appear above ground?

At about 10 to 12 days the cubs can regulate their own heat and their eyes are open. Unlike those of their parents, their eyes will be blue in colour. At this early stage of their lives the cubs will be very selfish with food and have been known to kill other cubs in fights to secure their share. After a month of kennelling in the earth, the cubs appear above ground, usually in early April.

The chocolate-brown coats give them an appearance of little bears. The cubs when above ground are at first very wary, and even the slightest noise will send them diving for cover. Through their mock fighting they learn many of the techniques that will aid them in later life both in securing food and a place in the pecking order. Most of the adult-to-adult interactions can be observed being performed in the young cubs: body slamming, the fox trot and even at this stage dominant and submissive postures are adopted.

The vixen, although she is still suckling her offspring, will by April be hunting for her cubs, as will the dog fox. At about 6 weeks of age the cubs will be losing their chocolate-brown coats and the adult colours will be starting to show through. Their small round heads will start to develop, their ears become erect and muzzles slightly more elongated.

At about 8 weeks the cubs will look more like little adults, and it is usually about this stage that the vixen will start to wean them. This may explain why she chooses to kennel away from her young, returning often during both day and night with solid food, possibly in the form of a dead rabbit or pigeon. It is the vixen's habit of lying away from her cubs that leads many people to think the cubs have been abandoned. The cubs may also go out hunting with other family members, and I have noted that the cubs appear to be split; in the case of 4, 2 with one parent, 2 with another.

By 3 months of age the cubs will be far more self-sufficient and, although they will travel with an adult through the night, most of the time they forage in pairs together. By about September the cubs are better described as sub-adults, and some may now even start to leave their natal areas.

Diet

I feel it is their diet that has been the foxes' ultimate success. It has made them such masters of adaptability that they thrive in most conditions whether urban or rural. Unlike some animals that specialise in just one food source, the fox will turn to almost anything for its diet, and some of the ways they secure their food are amazing.

To prepare for a time when food may be in short supply a fox will bury a surplus for a later date; this way of avoiding starvation is called 'cacheing'. Most people who feed foxes will note that a fox will fill its mouth and retreat, only to return minutes later to do it again, doing this many times until all the food is gone; mainly the larger items are cached. Even people who have lost a run full of chickens to a fox may have been the victim of the fox's cacheing technique.

People who have found all the chickens dead in their chicken coops, and only one actually eaten often think the fox kills for fun. This is not so, man is the only animal who kills for fun. A fox on entering a chicken coop will have come across an abundance of prey which cannot escape, something completely unnatural in the wild, so follows its instinct to chase something that is fleeing: an instinct that must come into play when there is the possibility of food. The fox will often return to the coop (when it may be met with a loaded gun) to cache the surplus. The same behaviour can be observed in a well fed cat. It will still stalk and kill a bird, even though it is not hungry. It has not done this out of a blood-lust. It is an instinct which can be observed also in our domestic dog; a dog will bury a bone, or can often be observed attempting to hide its food under a carpet when not hungry. An intelligent animal will secure food when it is available for future consumption.

Fox in typical pose, using the back teeth to crush peanuts.

A territory can provide many items of food for the fox, but not one of these can be relied upon. Myxomatosis was introduced to kill the rabbits and up to 99% of them were destroyed; the fox, which had until then had rabbit on the menu, did not suddenly starve; he just turned his attention to another food source. Earthworms may in some seasons of the year be abundant and foxes may spend the night scooping them up, but if they relied solely upon a diet of earthworms then in times of hot weather or drought they would starve. To describe the fox's diet, I would have to say anything goes! I have had phone calls complaining about urban foxes entering houses to steal the cat's food, reports of foxes walking up to patio windows, sitting down outside waiting for the householder to feed them. In every situation the fox has adapted, and adapted well.

Many people ask why has the fox come into our back gardens to live and breed, when it belongs in the countryside? But nobody questions the existence of hedgehogs or wild birds in towns. We leave peanuts and seed out for the birds; we leave saucers of water and dog food out for the hedgehogs. The area where I studied foxes is a typical example of what happens: for about three years I studied a fox family in a countryside environment. Their main diet at the time appeared to be rabbit, supplemented with voles, earthworms and fruit. If there is such a thing as the typical country fox I was studying it. Their earth was in a cover of trees and hedges, and the regular trails around the area suggested the area had been fox-occupied for some years. Then disaster struck. Planning permission was given for a housing estate of over one hundred and fifty houses. Soon the area of which I had grown fond was barren. The regular fox paths had been replaced with tarmac; the rabbit warren was flattened, and the trees and hedges which used to conceal the earth were cut down. My countryside retreat became a concrete jungle.

I worried about the foxes and what they would do for food and where they would breed. Yet the masters of adaptability not only survived but thrived. Within a very short time the householders in this area were asking why foxes, which belonged in the countryside, had started to invade their streets and gardens and had chosen earths under garden sheds to give birth! In fact the foxes were the original residents and the people invaded *their* territory.

Thankfully not all people view the urban fox with suspicion. Many now welcome it into their gardens. They provide food nightly, something which the fox has come to regard as the norm. The urban fox has done a lot to change people's views on foxes, because the urban fox is allowing itself to be observed by people who have never had the pleasure before. This beautiful, misunderstood animal is at last climbing the popularity ladder.

Enemy of the fox

In the balance of nature, the fox is top of the food chain, a food chain that ensures both predator and prey are kept in reasonable control. When myxomatosis nearly wiped out the rabbits (i.e. the fox's prey) the foxes did not starve because they turned their attention to other food sources, so even when there aren't enough prey items for the predator, the predator, as long as it's adaptable, will survive. Only animals that rely on one food source become extinct if that food source dwindles or dies out. If there is an epidemic of prey populations, then the predator numbers will rise in response to this; but such fluctuations in numbers are cyclical and the predator follows the downward as well as the upward cycles. Take away the predator and the whole ecosystem will suffer; take, for instance, the overpopulation of deer, resulting in unhealthy herds. This is because of the absence of the wolf, a predator which would prey on the weak and the sick deer, ensuring the herds were healthy, and kept down to reasonable numbers, providing enough good grazing for the remaining animals. Unfortunately the wolf was exterminated in this country. With the absence of the wolf, man now claims these herds of deer need controlling. They cull what they say are the old and the weak, they claim this needs to be done because of the absence of a natural predator! The fox, like the wolf, is a predator, but, like the wolf which used to roam our countryside, the fox is now persecuted under the misguided banner of control. Along with the control of the fox, using amongst other things, guns, snares and traps, we have another enemy of the fox: sport.

The enjoyment of galloping over the countryside and jumping hedges is fair enough, but unfortunately hunting also includes killing the fox. To make the excuse of this that hunting controls fox numbers is not valid since (a) hunting also claims to conserve foxes and (b) foxes control their own numbers. It is not in their interests to over breed, and the only time they possibly do so is when man upsets the finely balanced scales of nature. Our attempts to control foxes can actually result in an increase in their numbers.

Some diseases can be fatal to the fox such as mange and will limit numbers.

It is a sad fact that whilst a fox can live to the ripe old age of fourteen in captivity, the average lifespan for country and urban foxes does not often exceed eighteen months, and many do not live to celebrate their first birthday, as a direct result of man and his machines.

— 2 —
On the Fox's Trail

A knowledge of the area in which you are planning to set up observations is of paramount importance, as is getting the relevant permission to be on the land in the first place. Once you have gained the permission to be on the land night and day, you must then go about attempting to discover if foxes visit or, even better, actually live and breed in your selected area.

I cannot stress enough the importance of getting to know your chosen area by both day and night. At every available opportunity through the daylight hours you should be out walking across the land. Learning what lies behind a hedge or wall will, you probably think, do nothing to help you observe foxes. This may be the case but when you are successfully watching foxes, having an insight as to where they go when they disappear through these very hedges or around the walls is essential, and may give some indication of the size of the fox's territory.

Foxes will live in towns, cities and the countryside, so most places will have at least foxes visiting. Good places to look for them are: school playing fields, hospital grounds, waste land, fields, college and university grounds, cemeteries and golf courses. You could also ask the people most likely to see them to inform you where and when they do. These people could include milkmen, postmen, nurses, shift workers and security guards. Since many towns and cities now have surveillance cameras around the main centres, it may be worth asking if you could view these in case foxes have been caught on camera. Many companies also have their buildings watched by cameras; with the right approach from yourself they may be pleased to swap any videos they have featuring foxes for a blank supplied by you.

Assuming you have the permission needed, the next step is to discover if foxes are present on the land, or at the very least visit it. Once you have established that foxes do visit a particular spot, by detection of the signs, then the next thing to do is to decide on your best observation point. A hide is not necessary. I say that setting up an observation point is the easiest way, but, unless you have got the right place, the observation point will be useless. You may go out every night, sit in exactly the same place and wait for about the same amount of time, yet still observe nothing. You could easily be led to believe that the area you are watching does not contain foxes; but it is perfectly possible that the area you have chosen is one of the last fields the foxes visit in their night-time foraging. You will always miss them. Or you could even be watching the wrong side of the field. You may sit down your first time out and successfully watch a fox in the field you have chosen, but the best way of increasing your chances of success is to have a knowledge of the signs they leave behind: footprints, remains of previous kills and fox droppings.

This sounds easy enough, but, faced with a large ploughed field, where do you start? This is where having an insight into the fox's behaviour is important.

In this chapter I hope to help you not only to discover fox signs but also to know the best places in which to look for them.

Detecting the signs

During the daylight hours go out to your chosen area, stand for a while and survey the land. Is there a stream or river nearby which separates one field from another? Is there a wood? Is the field used to graze cattle or sheep? Is the field enclosed with hedges, or barbed wire fence? Draw a simple sketch of the field and any surrounding fields. Include as much detail as possible: rabbit warrens, badger setts.

Once your drawing is complete, go to the top of the field, and walk slowly down the perimeter fence, stopping often to check any bare soil. If the fence is barbed wire, check for tufts of hair entangled from when a fox may have crept underneath. The fox's hair will vary in colour and thickness depending largely on whether the fox has caught the hair on its back by moving under the fence, or if it has caught the hair on its stomach region by going over. The hair on the fox's back is usually grey/brown, whilst that from the under side can be predominantly white. If you are walking parallel to a stream, check to see if footprints go down to the water's edge, and, if they do, attempt to see if there are also prints the other side. It has often been said that foxes will use these water jumps only during the mating season, but from my experience I have found water jumps are used all year round.

The fox's fore feet are about the same size as those of a King Charles Spaniel, measuring about 6 centimetres(2.4 in) long by about 4 centimetres(1.5 in) wide. Closer inspection of the prints can usually determine if they are fox's or dog's, for the two middle toes of a fox are closer together at the front, with the two other toes set further back.

If you find any droppings check that they are those of a fox. The

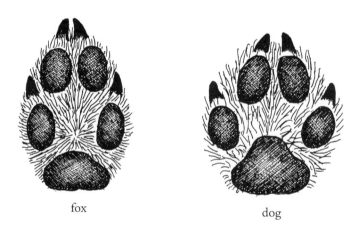

fox

dog

Comparison of fox and dog footprints.

most typical dropping will be about the size of a domestic small dog's, measuring about 10 centimetres(4 in) in length, with tapered ends. Bones, fur and feather as well as other insect remains will be visible. I have found in the latter part of the year when fruit such as blackberries and plums are abundant the consistency of the dropping resembles more that of a badger, or of a very small cowpat. For country foxes feeding on a diet of fruit, small mammals and birds, one can quite easily determine by eye alone that the dropping is that of a fox, for several recognisable items can be observed. The usual fox dropping is tapered at both ends, more so if it is mainly made up of rabbit. Small mammal hairs can be observed, as can grass, seeds, insect remains and small bones. After a couple of days I have found the sun bleaches white the droppings that usually contain more bones.

Foxes also feed on earthworms. Remains of these however can only be detected under a microscope: a subject covered later on in this book.

Urban fox droppings are a little harder to distinguish from those of a dog, simply because urban foxes are probably eating the same sort of diet as a dog, but if the dropping is still fresh, the distinct foxy odour should be easily detected.

Droppings are not used solely to rid the fox of its bodily waste; a fox will usually defecate in conspicuous places, that is conspicuous to other foxes. These droppings serve as another way of communicating either within families or with other neighbouring families. When foxes defecate the two anal glands situated just under the tail squeeze together secreting a fluid on to the dropping.

Fox droppings are usually found at more regular intervals along the borders of the territory, thus alerting neighbouring foxes to the fact that the area is occupied and will be defended. Fox droppings can also be found 'nose high' to mammals, such as on high tufts of grass, rocks and salt blocks. In urban areas garden ornaments are favoured. I feel that the purpose of these is not so much visual as olfactory: the idea is for any other fox to be assailed by the smell.

The droppings foxes use to inform neighbouring foxes to keep out

fox

badger

dog

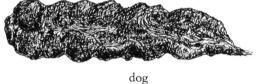

Comparisons of fox, badger and dog droppings.

are also used to communicate with members of their own families. I have often found in the middle of a fox's territory a complete rabbit warren marked with a dropping at every entrance. This leads me to conclude that within a territory there may be quite a number of good feeding grounds actually defended by a fox from members of its own family. Fox droppings can also be found on top of prey remains, so that all the fox detective finds at this spot are feathers and the fox's calling cards. I would assume that the droppings once again are used as a form of communication.

Foxes, being creatures of habit, are quick to notice if even a stone has been moved on their normal paths, or if a strange object is present. I have capitalised on this when collecting droppings for analysis by moving stones onto the fox's regular trails. They will usually leave droppings on top of them, or at the very least sprinkle the new items with urine.

The fox's urine can be usually detected around entrances to fields and on posts and other prominent positions. Describing the smell of the urine is almost impossible, but if I was to try, I suppose it smells very much like a freshly opened jar of Nescafé coffee, but do not tell Nescafé I said this! Once you have started to discover fox's droppings the unmistakable scent of the fox's urine is sure to hit the nostrils.

This is another way a fox communicates. It will have several marking posts in and around the territory where it sprinkles urine sparingly.

Fox trails can usually be detected along hedgerows, across meadows, across lawns and under fences. These trails will be used nightly, for the fox is most certainly a creature of habit. The trail will measure about 10 centimetres(4 in) wide, and in most cases will not be worn down to the bare earth, as is the case with a badger trail. With a fox's

Creatures of habit, foxes will use regular trails nightly.

trail, vegetation will be clear above about 60 centimetres (24 in). A badger's will be about 24 centimetres wide (10 in) and will be clear of vegetation above about 40 centimetres from the ground (15 in).

Trails across meadows are easily detected on the morning after a night's frost or even when the grass is wet with dew. In the latter case the grass shows signs of being bruised, much as when you walk across a field you can look back and see your own trails. Following these trails may lead you to a previous kill. You may find a dropping or catch the scent of the fox's urine. More importantly the trail may lead you into a copse where the animal sleeps for the day.

Most of these tracks, signs and trails are restricted to the borders of the fields. Knowing this saves time and effort spent walking across the middle of large fields, yet discovering nothing. If however the field is ploughed, it may be worth crossing by following the tracks left behind by the farmer's machinery; foxes will, it appears, always opt for the easier route. Why make a trail of your own if a human has done the hard work?

Discovering if the bird remains you have found are the fox left overs is usually quite simple: feathers show signs of being chewed at the base. In contrast, if the bird was killed by a sparrowhawk or other bird of prey, for example, the base of the feather will have a neat ring mark on it made from the bird's beak. Another way of determining if it is a fox's kill is if all that is left is the rib cage with the wings still attached. You may find a hedgehog skin that has been turned inside out, or even that of a rabbit when all that remains is a neatly cleaned skin. Both however could be the kill remains of a badger.

Mostly, foxes will choose to live above ground, lying up under hedges or in ditches; the vixen will choose an underground earth (or several) before her cubs are born. Knowing how to distinguish a fox's earth could ensure some successful watching of the fox cubs when they emerge for the first time from the earth's mouth.

The earth

In most fox territories a vixen will select two or three earths before giving birth. Having more than one ensures that the vixen has a backup should the earth she is using be disturbed. In the course of the vixen's selection of a suitable earth she may visit several holes and may even start excavating, yet not use them, so do not be fooled into thinking that because you have found a hole that has recently been excavated, and shows signs of footprints or droppings that this is the fox's earth. On discovering such a hole make sure you note down its position on your sketch of the area. I have found that within most fox territories the earth is usually situated quite close to water, and usually in the centre of the territory. A vixen will often use a rabbit hole which she will enlarge to suit her needs, and more often than not there will be more than one entrance/exit. This probably serves as a security measure. Foxes will on occasions co-habit with badgers, or may use an old disused badger tunnel.

A fox's earth with droppings marking the earth's mouth.

Although it is often said that fox's earths are easily discovered, I have found this not to be the case in the early part of the year when there are no cubs. A fox earth entrance is usually a little larger than a rabbit hole, yet a little smaller than a badger hole: about fifteen inches in diameter.

Determining whether the hole is that of a fox or badger is quite simple. A badger's sett usually comprises several holes with large spoil heaps; badgers are compulsive diggers. The immediate area will usually be worn down to the ground and balls of grass, straw or hay litter the outside. These balls are collected by the badger to line its sett and after use will be pulled out and left to air. Foxes do not use bedding of any description when giving birth so the cubs are born on the bare earth. Other signs to be found are the lacerations on the base of trees, often causing all the bark to be removed. Closer examinations of such trees show these to be the sharp claw marks left behind not by the fox but the badger.

Badger dung pits, latrines, can also be found. The badger is said to be a very clean mammal, hence the toilet area. They dig shallow holes and deposit their dung inside. It is thought that more than one badger will use the same area making it a communal latrine. I feel that these latrines, which are usually scattered around the badger's territory, serve more than a repository for dung. I believe these too could be ways the badger communicates with any neighbouring badgers. Another sign to look for to distinguish fox from badger is the badger's footprint: unlike that of the fox, which has four, the badger has five toes and very long and sharp claws, and, because the badger is a heavier mammal, badger trails are often worn down to the bare soil: whereas fox trails are not. Because fox and badger holes and droppings may be confused the trails are a good way of differentiating them.

By now your drawing should include many features of the area in which you are planning to watch, including the occurrence of fox droppings, prey remains, scratched trees, badger/fox hairs on barbed wire, badger setts, rabbit warrens, regular paths, even where you caught a whiff of a fox's urine. You should also have a greater insight into the fox's forag-

Barbed wire fences can often hold clues as to the animals that crawl under or over them.

ing grounds. The most likely places that the fox may choose in which to lie up during the day are your first most important discoveries.

Discovering these is most important because foxes will leave these areas every day at dusk and return to them at dawn. This will put you one step ahead of the fox, and then all you have to do is ensure you are sitting quietly at dusk or dawn to view the fox either leaving on its night-time foraging, or returning from it. In your selection of a site to watch foxes avoid watching an area that contains mainly ploughed fields, as the fox will be camouflaged against the dark earth making observations difficult.

3

Aids to Successful Watching

What you need

Assuming Chapter 2 has given you an insight into the tracks and trails left behind by the night-time wanderings of the secret fox, and assuming you have found some, if not all, of these signs in your selected area, the next step is actually to go out into the field to discover if your homework has given you the result you were after: successful foxwatching.

I have found the best time to watch foxes leaving their day-time sleeping quarters is just before dusk or around dawn; time obviously varies in accordance with the season. Before going out into the field, ensure you have the right equipment, the price of which need not run into hundreds of pounds; it really does not need to go over £30.

The most essential pieces of equipment for the fox watcher are binoculars, but with so many models on the market which ones do you choose? Having tried numerous models in the field I feel happy with a pair of 10 x 8. You could be tempted into spending an extra £50 or so, in the belief that binoculars with a zoom feature will be useful. In certain cases this may be so, but mostly when you are out foxwatching the zoom feature will be ineffective, because of the lack of light. When purchasing your binoculars always ask for a good light-gathering pair. Prices usually start at around £25. At this point it is worth remembering that the success of your foxwatching will not rest upon what equipment you have, but rather it is the knowledge of the animal you are watching that will pay dividends. So do not worry if a lot of the good equipment is out of your financial reach.

You will be surprised at just how much you will have forgotten by the time you reach home; writing whilst watching has never proved practical to me, so another handy piece of equipment is a dictaphone, not essential but useful, especially if you plan to record what you see including times and dates.

I have found several thin layers of clothes, topped by an army style green jumper and jacket, sufficient to keep me warm, even on the coldest of nights. A hot water bottle (stuffed down the jumper) is not unheard of in the colder months. Not only will you be warm, you will also be well camouflaged. To add to the camouflage and your warmth, a pair of gloves is recommended; although you might think fingerless ones would enable you to operate any equipment, I have found them unnecessary as well as uncomfortable; if your fingers are cold, you will feel colder, and if you only have binoculars with you, the only fiddling you need to do – focussing – can be done with gloves. The finish to the camouflage you may think would be a balaclava: to give a warm face and a concealed one. But if you have ever attempted to wear a balaclava and watch through binoculars at the same time, you will realize the two do not often go together; in most cases the binoculars will steam up, and most of your time will be spent in de-misting them. What I suggest is an old hat and a piece of scrim (green net) which can be tied around the back of the neck and pulled up around the mouth and nose. The binoculars will not steam up because of the small holes in the scrim. The most obvious choice of clothes, yet noisiest, worn by many people I have taken out foxwatching are waterproof jacket and trousers. You will realise exactly what I mean if you have ever walked quietly behind someone in the field who has chosen to wear these articles. The noise that comes just from the trousers when the person walks is enough to scare away the deafest of foxes. Even when sitting in one position quietly, I can shut my eyes yet still be able to tell how many times my companions have lifted their binoculars to their eyes and back again. Waterproofs are ideal wear during bad weather doing field studies, but I would certainly not recommend them for actual watching. All these clothes can be purchased at a reasonable price at the army surplus stores or alternatively you could dye some of your own old clothes.

The finishing touches are a pair of comfortable shoes; I do not favour wellington boots for I have found however much you attempt to creep, your wellies make a noise. Shoes or boots are really a matter of personal preference, but always try to go for either black or brown and the quieter the better.

The one piece of equipment I have so far failed to mention is the camera. My reasons I hope will become clear. Firstly, until you have watched successfully for at least a month, I would recommend the camera stays at home. It is so easy to become trigger happy or should I say shutter happy, when one first views a fox, thus making the fox bolt for the nearest cover, and wasting maybe hours of watching – for a picture that will probably turn out blurred anyway, if it turns out at all! I have found the best photographic opportunities occur when the cubs are first above ground and when you have learnt how to attract the foxes to you, something I will discuss in more detail further on in this chapter.

Taking up your post

The most precious of all qualities now is patience. You could be the best camouflaged person ever to step out into the field to watch and study foxes but if you have no patience and decide to move about after an hour of unsuccessful watching or, worse, decide to go home, you may as well have been dressed in a metallic silver suit with a ghetto blaster for a companion. If you have not got the slightest bit of patience, rather than going home early, do not bother even going out in the first place; only patience will be rewarded.

By now the reason I suggested you go into your chosen area through daylight hours as many times as possible should be becoming clearer. It was not just simply to find tracks and trails left by the foxes, but also because after spending days out in the field you should have located several good observation areas, maybe under a tree or next to a wall. Obviously the best place to set up your watching place will be not too far from the area where you believe the foxes could be lying up during the day. Another good reason for your day-time excursions was so you could not only get the feel of the land, but also identify the best places to avoid in the darkness such as slippery banks. Do not start watching until you are sure you know the land well enough to move about in the darkness.

It is also good practice to alert friends or family as to where you are going and roughly what time to expect you back. At least then if anything were to happen, you could be located.

Never make the mistake of believing that because the weather is reasonably warm, you can leave off a couple of articles of clothing. One thing is sure: when darkness falls, so does the temperature, and sitting in one spot for hours upon end always makes you feel colder.

Wherever you have decided to set up your observation point, always get there at least an hour before darkness falls, or if you are morning watching an hour before sun-rise. Your approach to, and departure from, your vantage point should always be done as quietly as possible.

When selecting a site for observation you should always consider the possibility of rain. Although being out in the middle of a field may give you some good observation, always use possible cover such as isolated trees or bushes to break the familiar human form; try squatting or sitting down in front of something that will break up your outline. Once in your selected place get yourself as comfortable as possible and pass the time waiting for the foxes by looking across the field whilst the light is still available, discounting any object that will appear to be a fox when the light fails. Believe me, when foxwatching the eyes are sure to play tricks and the mind always seems willing to believe them. Even a tuft of grass can fool you into believing that it is a fox. The more you stare, the more you believe the tuft is actually moving. You can even start seeing fox-like ears perched on top. Stare a little harder and you are sure to make out the fox's brush. To ensure you don't spend all night grass-tuft watching, note the position of all unusual looking objects. It is worth remembering that most foxes are on the move within seconds, so if the object has failed to move, discount it.

There are times however when a fox may just sit down and stare for ages into the night, and some choose to sleep in the middle of a field. Having said this most of your foxwatching observations will be of foxes on the move, especially if they have just woken from their day-time sleep.

When the darkness starts to fall, your eyes should become accustomed quite naturally, and you will be surprised by how much you can see. I honestly believe the more times you are out in the darkness, the better your eyesight becomes. People who have been out foxwatching with me always comment on how good my eyes must be. After finishing my watching for the night I often walk across the field, look back and am amazed by how dark it really was out there.

After a time, if your first observations have been correct, a fox should emerge from the area you expected. Usually before setting off into the night a fox will sit for a couple of minutes surveying the immediate area, and then almost as if it has been whistled, it will be off, seemingly in a straight line, stopping only occasionally to investigate a clump of grass, or mark a certain area.

It should now become obvious why foxwatching over ploughed fields has its drawbacks, for the fox almost disappears against the brown earth; it is better if you have managed to select an area of meadow. The biggest give away to a fox is movement, and an over ambitious swing with the binoculars from your waist to your eyes has been known to send a fox bolting for cover even a field away. On viewing a fox, if the binoculars are not near to eye, bring them up with a smooth and slow action. This also applies when moving or turning around. If you have to move, do so only when the fox is not looking in your direction.

After watching the fox go across the field, always remember from where it first appeared. Check back to this area with your binoculars regularly, for I have found that most of the fox family when leaving an area of cover will follow the same path as the other foxes. This will not only give you further foxwatching opportunities but it will also give some indication of the number of members within the fox group.

Record such details as white tips to tails, any distinguishing marks that would help you recognize the same fox again, the times each fox appeared, the direction each fox has taken, any interactions between two or more foxes and especially the day and date. I find it useful to photocopy outlines of foxes and take these with me when foxwatching. I can then mark the distinguishing features of the foxes on these pictures. You may also hear some calls of foxes. Note these down as well, giving a brief description of the calls heard. These notes will become the basis of your study and I have found it best to record them in diary form, by the day rather than by the month. You will be surprised when looking back after a couple of months how these records can help you in the coming weeks, months and years of foxwatching. At this point it is best not to put names to individual foxes. I made this mistake in my first year of watching, calling a fox 'Shadow' because he appeared darker than the others I had observed, only to discover later three or four Shadows in the group. The biggest mistake I made was in calling a fox 'Two-Tone' because of the apparent two-tone coloured coat, only to discover after three to four months that most of the foxes had this two-tone appearance because of the moulting process. This made my first few months of notes highly inaccurate. Name a fox only if you are 100% sure you will be able to identify it again. Remember, just because you have had the privilege of observing maybe three different foxes and all three had different markings you may think you can name them accordingly, but what happens if another three or four foxes from the same family group were foraging in another field out of sight? These could have virtually the same markings, making your notes inaccurate to say the least. So at this point I would recommend you just detail what you see rather than choosing names. Later on in this chapter I will discuss how to attract the foxes to you. You may then have a better opportunity to observe the subtle differences between family members, and so be able to give specific names with a degree of accuracy.

It is worth keeping an ear out for bird warning calls when a fox moves past a tree or hedgerow, for being able to detect these calls is to your advantage. Many times a bird has given out a warning cry minutes before I have actually observed a fox.

If on your first night out you were lucky enough to observe foxes for some time, excellent, but what happens if you failed to find one at all? Go back through the stages set out earlier, until you get it right. Patience will be rewarded. What if you waited for about an hour or so only to have about six minutes of watching? Do not worry. Having watched a fox for a minute will have proven to you that your fieldwork has paid off, albeit for a very short time.

Now is the time for reflection. You have gone out into the field in daylight; you have studied the field intimately; you have noted down all tracks and signs; you have made a decision on where you thought the best place from which to watch would be; you have gone out into this very field and had the pleasure of watching your fieldwork come together for you have observed your fox. In doing so you have managed to become one step ahead of the fox. Do not at this point attempt to run before you can walk; don't be tempted to move to a vantage point nearer to where the foxes come out, in the hope of closer observation.

For the next few weeks, return to the same spot on every occasion. Attempt to discover the area the foxes are heading for, and what they are doing when they get there. Note down the closest point the foxes cross to you. You have had patience so far in your field studies. Do not start getting impatient now, for it is only after the first few weeks, possibly months, that you will be nearing the end of your foxwatching apprenticeship, and, believe me, this is when the fun really starts.

Enticing the foxes

Check your nightly fox diary for the nearest point they passed to your observation area. It does not matter if this is forty feet away or a whole field. What matters is that you have noted the position with some accuracy.

When you are confident you have found the nearest point, take a bag of food on your next visit. This can contain leftovers from your dinner, fruit, dog food, raisins, peanuts or bread. All you need is about a quarter of a carrier bagful of food.

Arrive with your food at your normal time, that is one hour before nightfall or sun-rise. Take the food and empty the contents around the area you have plotted. To increase your observation of the foxes feeding, do not put out large items of food such as whole chicken carcasses or half a loaf of bread because if and when the foxes find the food, your only observation will be of a fox picking up the large items and retreating somewhere quiet to devour them. Always break down large items, in addition scatter raisins and dog biscuits around.

This will then with luck keep the foxes feeding for a longer time in your selected area. Once you have emptied the contents, return quickly and quietly to your observation point and wait.

If you have plotted the crossing point with accuracy, it will only be a matter of time before the foxes discover your offerings. Do not be dismayed however if when the foxes find the food they retreat at speed. It may be your scent on the food. If this does happen check first thing in the morning to see if your food has been taken. If it has, all well and good. If it remains do not worry, it will be taken. If you have been fortunate enough to have the foxes feeding from the site, excellent, things can now only get better. Because foxes selfishly do not share food with other members of their family, I would suggest that you scatter it around a ten-foot radius. This may then ensure that more than one fox will feed without being too close to each other. Do not just empty the contents of the bag in one heap.

When foxes come across an abundance of food you may see them taking food away and cacheing it. Cacheing is the process of burying food for a later date. Many other animals cache surplus food to ensure that when food or prey is short they have got a supply in reserve. Even the domestic dog can be observed cacheing a favourite bone in the garden. In the domestic dog however this may not be a life or death matter, for food is always available, whereas for the fox and other wild animals this instinct could make the difference between eating and starving.

If you provide food regularly, the foxes will soon learn where to come for an easy and available meal. Try to supply it on a nightly basis. Even if you plan not to watch one night it would take only a minute to drop the food at the regular site.

The more fieldwork you are willing to put in, the more enjoyment you will ultimately get out.

After a couple of weeks, when the foxes are visiting the site regularly, move the food site about ten to fifteen feet closer to your observation point. Leave a small trail of food from the old to the new site, thus ensuring they find it with ease. By now your direct observations of foxes should have greatly increased. If they have not, do not despair. Just go back through the early stages until you get it right. Your main goal in tempting the foxes towards you should be to get them feeding in the brightest part of the field, so providing better observations.

Be sure to be note down exactly what you see, rather than what you think you see. Keep your notes as accurate as possible. After a couple of weeks at the new food site, repeat the same actions until you eventually manage to get the foxes feeding from about twenty to thirty feet away. At this point do not blow all your hard work by attempting to encourage the foxes to come too close. Twenty to thirty feet away should be quite close enough. If you find you have moved the food too close and the foxes are too nervous to feed, do not feel you have failed. You may have to move the food site back a few feet; getting it right is what counts.

Whatever distance the food site is away from you, the foxes will still be showing signs of extreme caution, crawling almost on their bellies only to grab a morsel of food and retreating as quickly as possible. If you do not move or make a sound the foxes will eventually realise there is nothing to fear and return each time all the braver. Once the food starts to dwindle, if there is more than one fox present, you may observe several squabbles. This may then give you an indication of the particular fox's social rank within the group.

After a month or so you should have a food site that is easily observed, and visited regularly by the resident fox or foxes. When watching foxes feeding close to you, it is easy to become fixed on their eyes, so when they go, you haven't got any identification markings. Whilst this may seem a strange thing to say, believe me, you will do it for the first couple of times without even noticing. You must make a conscious effort every time you see a fox to scan the body for markings that may prove good for identification.

By bringing the food with you and subsequently to the foxes, you have made foxwatching that much easier. You have cut out the hard work of attempting to trail a fox across fields. Now your time can be spent watching foxes rather than merely looking for them. Your notes should prove to be a lot more exciting to read than before. You may even be able to identify several different family members. You may also have an insight into their social ranks. From now on you will be learning all the time. When you begin to get a little blasé about the foxes at your food site, just think back to when a glimpse of a fox's silhouette against the night sky was enough to reward hours of patient waiting, I am sure you will then appreciate your hard work and dedication and the benefits they have reaped. You should have now discovered that buying and constructing a hide would be of no benefit. Image Intensifiers (which enable the viewer to see in the dark) will also be of no use. If you have done your fieldwork right the foxes should be easily observed without the need to spend hundreds of pounds. All you really need successfully to watch foxes are a pair of light gathering binoculars and a lot of patience.

Photography

Once you have managed to identify some of the individual foxes, not just by differences in colour but also in behaviour, you may like to try your hand at a little photography. Adding photographs to your diary is a good way of keeping it interesting. You may notice different markings of the photographed fox that you failed to notice by eye alone, and you can build up a collection of pictures of the individual foxes in the family you are studying.

A single lens reflex camera is by far the best choice. Interchangeable lenses offer a lens almost for every occasion. I have found the best all-round lens is the 70-210 zoom lens. This enables framing of a subject with ease. You could spend hundreds of pounds on a camera and subsequently hundreds of pounds on different lenses to fit it. Only go for what you can afford. It's not what you have got, it's the way that you use it that counts. Whether you have chosen the cheapest S.L.R. on the market or you have opted for the latest model, you are sure to get acceptable results with either.

Whilst tripods are cumbersome, they can ultimately make or break a photograph. At the very least you should invest in a sturdy monopod. This is where the more you spend the better quality you get applies. A simple flash gun set to the side of the camera is usually adequate. I suggest the flash set to the side of the camera because this usually cuts down the chance of a fox picture with big white eyes.

If you have a shiny metallic finish to your camera, tripod or monopod, cover this up with more green scrim. This will ensure no shiny surfaces will be noticed by the visiting foxes. I choose to load the camera with 400 asa film, which I feel gives good all round performance at both dusk and dawn.

Once your camera is set up and ready to go, leave the flash off until you notice a fox coming towards the food site. This will ensure that at the moment you need to fire your flash, there is enough power in it to do so. Another advantage of bringing the fox to you, and encouraging it into the lightest part of the field is that focussing on the foxes when they arrive will prove to be less of a hit or miss affair. Before the foxes do visit it is worth getting your lens focussed on the area, then when the foxes do arrive only a few changes will need to be made. You will probably find that when you take the first photograph the sound of your camera clicking and the flash of light will send every fox in the district scurrying for cover. Do not move at this point. Just wind on to the next frame as quickly and as quietly as possible.

On most occasions the foxes will return when they feel the danger has passed. They soon learn that there is nothing to fear from flash lights. Do not feel you have to take your camera every time, for too many clicks and flashes could discourage the foxes from feeding. Once or twice a week I feel is ample.

There are other ways of encouraging the foxes to you while out in the field, but be sure these are a good distance away from the food site. Bring along a torch or a lamp as well as a child's squeaky toy and, rather than settling down in your usual observation point, choose a field nearby. Then crouch against a fence, tree or some other concealed spot and shine your torch around. The torch need not be a powerful one – just enough to shine about halfway across the field. If any foxes are present they will be easily identified because their eyes will shine back with an orange light, like two small torches. On discovering a fox is in the field, start to squeeze your squeaky toy; usually the squealing of the toy will be enough to arouse the curiosity of the fox which will start to make its way towards your position. Sometimes it will come in a direct line but most of the time will semi-circle its way over. In doing so I feel the foxes are attempting to catch any scent available, so it is a good idea to be sitting down-wind when possible. The squeaky toy is to fool the fox into thinking that a rabbit or other animal is in distress. The same noise can be made by sucking one's hand until the desired pitch is reached.

Foxes will soon learn that the noises you are making do not bring them food, so if you are to use this method in attempting to photograph the foxes, do so over a couple of days before they become accustomed to the noise.

I have also had many foxwatching hours using a powerful one million candle power lamp. This has proved successful in some areas and not others, and please note if you know that foxes are shot in this area using a lamp, do not use one. You may be helping the shooters by getting the fox accustomed to and unafraid of the white light. I cannot stress this too much.

When I take out a lamp I first locate the foxes in the field, and when the nearest one is located I walk slowly towards it with the lamp on full beam. It is for this reason I use a powerful light, because the foxes are unable to see me behind it. It is possible to get within about fifteen feet of a fox foraging for worms and insects unnoticed. I then crouch down and watch. At this distance it is very easy to get some accurate identification as well as long observation of the feeding foxes. A quiet approach is a must.

In your attempt to stay one step ahead of the foxes, having an insight into what the foxes may be up to within each month of the year is helpful, hence the next chapter: Calendar of Events.

Overall do not do anything that you feel could disturb the foxes or place them in any danger.

Garden foxwatching

If you are aware that there are foxes in your area, or you back onto fields, playing fields, open spaces, the chances are that if the foxes are not actually using your garden, at least they will be coming quite close. A lot of people who have security lights have been wakened by them and have jumped out of bed expecting a human intruder – to be pleasantly surprised when they observe a fox looking back at them.

The way to encourage the foxes to visit your garden or spend more time in it is not to put out dog or cat food for them. If you do this you will find half the neighbourhood's cats feeding in your garden Start by throwing down two or three handfuls of raisins and a couple of slices of bread and jam cut up into small pieces; cats are not interested in either, but the fox will love both! I suggest bread mainly because it will be easily seen from your window, so you know where to look. Put the food near to the perimeter fence for the first week, or until you know that the foxes are certainly coming to feed. This is to build up their courage and also to get them used to the regular supply of food.

After you are sure the food is going to the foxes, you can create a food site nearer your house; ideally in the brightest part of the garden. Leave a trail of food from the old site to the new, just to ensure the foxes will find it easily. If the foxes are coming in the early hours, be patient, once they are aware that there is a regular food supply to be had they will start coming earlier. You may find that once the fox or foxes start visiting regularly, you can set your clocks by them; but if they suddenly start coming later, do not despair. I have found the best thing to do is to stop feeding them for one night after this. Then the next night you will usually find the foxes waiting for you, rather than you for them. I think this is possibly because when the fox visited on the night when there was no food, it obviously thought something else had got to the food first, and, to ensure this didn't happen again, it got there earlier the next night. Whether this is the right reason or not, it usually works.

Always remember that the foxes were surviving nicely without your food offerings, so do not make the mistake of increasing the food you supply because of the presence of cubs or more adults. I say this because in any fox territory the available food supply mirrors the fox numbers, so by increasing your offerings, you could actually increase the number of foxes in your area to an unnatural level. If you have more than one fox visiting just put down another couple of handfuls of raisins.

I have lost count of the number of the phone calls I have received from householders who, when they see fox cubs in their gardens, decide to feed them; then after a month or so they realise the damage and mess foxes can cause, and want to know how to deter them! The easiest way of deterring foxes is not to attract them in the first place. So if you are a keen gardener and worship your lawn and flower beds, bear this in mind before you start feeding the foxes.

When feeding foxes, many householders will place the food out on a tray or saucer, only to be disgusted when the fox, after feeding, squats over the plate and leaves them a calling card. If the idea of cleaning a fox dropping off a plate turns your stomach, then it may be best to avoid using trays and plates in the first place.

The only disadvantage of watching the foxes in your garden is that there is a tendency to see more foxes than there actually are. Since the foxes will go out one way and come in another, unseen, this one fox may be counted as two, so you can imagine just how many foxes you will think you observe when a vixen with five fox cubs turns up to eat.

Disadvantages of feeding foxes in your garden

Since your garden will be regarded by the foxes as a safe area, you may find that all the items the adults and cubs have pinched from other people's gardens – their shoes, dog bowls, etc – will be brought back to your garden. Trying to explain to your neighbours why one of their trainers is half buried in your flower bed can be a little embarrassing to say the least. Not all your neighbours will see you as the kind person who feeds wildlife when the foxes do something destructive in their gardens, so be prepared to take the stick. Although they are wild animals belonging to nobody, when they are causing problems, believe me, they will be your foxes. Many people will be against what you are doing, blaming you for encouraging the foxes in the first place. Sometimes you can persuade anti-fox neighbours to be more friendly by telling a little white lie. For instance, 'Do you know, I saw a fox chasing a big brown rat in your garden last night?' It is also worth pointing out to anyone who is against the feeding of foxes that whilst you are feeding them you are keeping them out of their gardens. Really this paragraph should be headed 'Disadvantages of having neighbours that do not feed foxes' – but perhaps I am biassed.

Backgarden photography

Householders who have outside lights often spend their time straining their eyes to see the foxes because they feel that turning on the lights will frighten them away. If you have an outside light, I suggest that you put it on thirty minutes before the foxes are expected. Leave the majority of the food in the shadows and place the best items, i.e. bread and jam sandwiches, in the light. For the first couple of nights you will possibly see the fox creeping around the shadows and darting in and out of the light area to get the best food. Once the fox appears quite calm about feeding on the bread and jam you can start to place all the food in the light area.

Watching from the house always gives the best photographic opportunities, since you are able to put the food where you want the fox. Then you just sit back in your chair in the warmth – and wait. Depending on the strength of the outside lights, a 400 asa film loaded in your camera may be enough without having to use a flash. To be on the safe side, take a light meter reading from the area where you plan to photograph the fox.

When using flash, the biggest mistake people often make is standing back indoors and taking a photograph through the window. When you get your photographs back the only thing that will be in the photographs will be your window frame and a mirror image of yourself! If you must use flash, ensure the flash gun is pressed right up to the window, and that there are no lights on behind you. The best results with flash are often achieved by rigging your flash gun up outside via a cable to the camera.

A sick fox

Often people who are feeding foxes either from their gardens or a food site feel helpless when they observe a fox with a very bad limp, or infected with mange.

Sprains and broken limbs

Most foxes will at some time in their short life sprain or hurt their legs. If you have a fox that is visiting and holding its leg off the ground, it is most certainly worth monitoring and in a lot of cases treating. The first thing to look out for is whether the fox is occasionally putting the foot to the ground. If this is the case it may suggest that the leg or foot is only sprained and not broken. In some cases with a bad sprain the fox will not put the leg to the ground at all, and it will hold it up under its body, hobbling around on three legs. In some cases, when the fox is in a lot of pain and discomfort, do not be surprised if you fail to see this particular fox for several nights. It seems that they lay up until the injury is better.

If the leg is broken, then it may be dragged, or if the fox is able to hold its leg off the ground, then you may see the leg flapping unusually. Sometimes with a bad break and swelling the leg may just be sticking out at an unusual angle. If you suspect that the leg is broken, then phone the National Fox Welfare Society (see useful addresses) and they will arrange to cage trap the fox with the injury and help it.

If you monitor the fox with the limp and feel satisfied that the fox hasn't got a broken leg, merely a sprained one, then you could give Arnica 30c, a homeopathic remedy that will aid recovery by treating any bruising; put 6 drops a day into a jam sandwich so that cats do not eat it. Do not be temped to treat an animal with medication meant for humans, for some can actually kill rather than cure.

Mange

The first signs of mange are that the fox will scratch continually, and whilst mange can affect any part of the body, it usually starts at the tail end and works its way up. Even today, foxes infected with mange are destroyed because it is felt to be the kindest thing to do, by putting the fox out of its misery. In my view, it's like considering euthanasia for someone with eczema: if a condition can be treated, then it should be. And mange, thankfully, can be treated.

The mange is caused by a tiny mite (*Sarcoptes scabei*) that burrows under the skin and multiplies. The irritation caused by the mite is severe, causing the fox to bite, lick and scratch the infected area. The area will have small pimples in the early stages and the pimples then become scabby. Bare, almost shaved looking patches will show around the body as a result of the hair having been bitten or scratched out. In untreated or heavily infected foxes, a musty odour is characteristic along with a thickening of the skin, giving the skin a folded appearance. Untreated, the fox will lose most of its hair and eventually die. It has also been noted that a fox with more than 50% of its body hair lost may also show symptoms of conjunctivitis.

The conventional medicine used to treat wild foxes has many drawbacks, the biggest one being that it is not readily available to the general public. It can also prove fatal to some breeds of dog if accidentally taken. So what other treatment is there? The National Fox Welfare Society is having great results with a homeopathic remedy. The beauty of any natural remedy is that there is no danger to a non-infected fox or other animal, i.e. cat or dog, and no danger of overdosing and no adverse side effects. The remedy (*Arsenicum album* and Suphur 30c) is said to work best if used in water, but, as many foxwatchers have found out, you very rarely see a fox drink. The same results have been obtained by placing the treatment on food. I would suggest that 3 drops a day are placed into jam or peanut butter sandwiches. Cats are not interested in sandwiches so will not rob the fox of its treatment. If more than one fox with mange is visiting, make several sandwiches, putting 10-12 drops out in all, and then scatter the sandwiches around the site. This will then ensure that each fox can feed without being nose to nose with any other fox, and each fox will receive the 3 drops necessary. Once again, do not worry if one fox takes two doses, you cannot overdose with this. Along with the mange, the remedy will also treat any signs of conjunctivitis.

Every year I take hundreds of calls from people either complaining about mangy foxes or from people concerned about their welfare. However, most of the reported foxes with mange are nothing more than foxes going through their natural moult. Most people view the fox's coat as bushy, so when they see a fox who has gone through its moult, they assume there is something wrong with the animal. It looks scruffy, so it must have mange. In some cases the hair appears to be coming out in clumps, but with mange the skin would be showing through underneath. The town fox is, and will probably always be, described as a 'mangy fox'. I feel the answer is in the fact that since more people are regularly seeing foxes in built-up areas, not only do they get to see a fox in full coat, but also foxes that are undergoing or have undergone the moult. To add to the confusion about the coat of the fox, most picture postcards of foxes show the fox in its winter coat, maybe to give the fox cuddly appeal, or possibly because photos of foxes come from colder parts of the world.

The homeopathic remedies mentioned can be obtained by contacting Helios Homeopathic Pharmacy (see Useful Addresses). If in doubt about any homeopathic treatment that you would like to give to visiting foxes, it is always worth phoning Helios and asking the relevant questions, the experiencd staff seem only too pleased to advise on the best remedy.

By treating a fox homeopathically, you get the satisfaction of watching an animal get better. You have the peace of mind that the treatment you are using will be of no danger to any other animal. You have also, through your actions, prevented a lot of stress for the fox or foxes, by avoiding the need to take them out of their natural environment. You may be, as I was, sceptical to say the least about treating with a homeopathic remedy, but I would suggest you do not criticise until you have tried it. I have sent out hundreds of treatments now for mange, and in almost all cases treatment has been a success.

━━━━ 4 ━━━━
Calendar of Events

Just as important as knowing how and where to watch and study foxes is knowing what the foxes' activities are in each month of the year. Some months, the foxes' day-time activities will increase and their departure from their day-time sleeping areas will be much earlier than usual. So if you are not aware of this change in the foxes' social life you could wait patiently for hours yet be unrewarded.

In certain months you could watch fox cubs at play in an area selected by their parents, whilst in other months you might wait patiently for hours without observing anything. With a little knowledge of the foxes' activities, you will increase your chances of successful watching and your understanding of the fox family you are studying. Not only will I attempt to give some indication of what to expect from the foxes' activities within each month of the year but also an indication of what to expect at the site where you place food.

You may read different accounts of fox activities elsewhere; here I offer you the fruits of my experience.

January

Nearly every month of the year you may have been out to your area with a view to doing a field study, but January, although cold and wet, to the fox detective is by far the most rewarding and educative month of the year. January is the month of unrest for the fox family. Not only is it the peak mating season, but it is also the peak dispersal season, when last year's offspring as well as some of the resident older foxes become unsettled and leave to find a territory and a mate of their own. Earths in your area should now be showing signs of being used, most probably by the vixen in anticipation of the mating season and her forthcoming litter. The resident dog fox will be defending and defining his territory, vocally and physically, from the neighbouring foxes. The vixen will be patrolling the territory's boundaries leaving her scent along the way in order to attract a mate.

Field edges will be showing a high concentration of footprints and droppings and a smell of fox urine will often be detected. Because of this increase in activity by both sexes separately along the borders of the territory, observations of two or more foxes together will be few and far between. To compensate for this lack of physical contact, the foxes will be communicating via a series of vocal calls. Dog foxes will be very vocal in their attempts to deter any wandering males away from the occupied territory and vixens will be calling to actively encourage the same wandering males. The contact call is either a single bark or a triple bark. Both sexes will also use the scream-like call in the mating season. Last year's cubs, now adults, may also be heard calling, in their attempts to attract a mate. Noting the area from which you hear the calls and plotting them on your map could give you an insight into the range of the territory.

It is in this month that day-time activity increases, so do not limit your watching just to evenings or mornings. Evening activity usually starts at around 6.00pm in the quieter areas, and the calls of the foxes can usually be heard until around 10.00pm. There then seems to be a rest period until about 3.00am and the calls start again until just before dawn.

The latter half of the month I have found is usually the best time to observe the dog fox trailing behind the vixen in his attempt to mate. If you do observe this, by adding 53 days you can normally be quite accurate in predicting when the cubs will be born. Foxes will visit your food site, albeit very sporadically, and I have found in the early part of the month it is usually only one fox at a time and this is usually the same one every night.

February

Snow may fall in any of the winter months and you should most certainly make use of the good tracking conditions it brings. I have found that after a night's snow, foxes can still be observed in the fields at 9.00am. By following snow trails you may find two pairs of tracks together especially in the early part of February. These I think are from the breeding foxes still remaining close after mating. After a little detective work it is possible to discover whether the trails you are following are those of a dog fox or vixen. Dog foxes will urinate by cocking their legs, sprinkling the urine to the left or the right of the tracks, whereas the vixen squats, sprinkling her urine behind her.

In the early part of this month vocal calls are still frequent; other signs are less so. Most droppings can now be found around the area of the breeding earth.

By this time the vixen will be using an earth in preparation for the birth of her cubs, and the earth will show signs of use. You may be tempted to watch the earth's mouth at dusk and dawn, but I would certainly not recommend this. If you are fortunate enough to observe the vixen leaving her earth, that is basically it, normally just a fleeting glimpse, but if the vixen detects your presence you may force her to abandon her earth. I recommend watching the earth only when the chance of observing cubs is high, something I will discuss in detail later on in this chapter.

This month for the foxes is much more relaxed and although foxes will disperse at any time of the year, most of those that were going to disperse will now have done so. The vixen should now be pregnant and the resident dog fox will be taking it easy. If only one fox has been visiting the food site up to now, you may observe two or more doing so together.

Foxes will start to forage at around 5.30pm, and if you have not yet discovered the whereabouts of the earth, watching at this time may give you some indication, for the dog fox will sleep not too far away.

March

The vixen will be usually confined to her earth ready to give birth to her cubs. Although March is the peak cubbing season early litters have been recorded, some even as early as January and February. If you do visit the area of the earth in the day be sure not to stay too long in the vicinity, because your scent may force the vixen to move to another earth.

Dog foxes will be more active, not only in feeding themselves, but also supplying the vixen with food. In quiet areas sometimes the vixen can be heard calling from the earth's mouth, calling her mate possibly through hunger.

Visits to the food site by more than one fox will be quite common, and it is certainly worth keeping an eye open for the dog fox, for he often can be observed taking advantage of a food site in this month. Some of the dog foxes I have observed over the years in March appear lethargic, suggesting that maybe by March they deserve a well earned rest.

Grooming forms an important part of the fox's social life, and helps to form bonds with individual family members.

April

Even in April, regular marking trails can be observed; droppings litter rabbit warrens and other food supplies. The foxes emerge a little later now, usually around 7.00pm, and can still be observed foraging at 7.00am in the morning. Fox cubs can often be observed in the early part of this month at the earth's mouth any time throughout the day; sunny warm mornings particularly lure them out. This provides an excellent opportunity to take photographs, and if the fox cubs are frightened by your presence and retreat into the earth, they will usually emerge fairly soon. At this point, however, do not be tempted to move too close, for the vixen willprobably still be kennelled with them. At your feeding site an increase in activity is usually noticed, sometimes as many as four or five foxes feeding at once. Aggressive and submissive postures are adopted frequently when the food you supplied begins to dwindle, so be sure to scatter your offerings around quite a large radius. Observing these interactions when they do happen may provide you with clues as to each fox's status within the family group.

April really is the worst time to name any adult foxes you observe at your feeding site. The reason becomes apparent when you realise that the adult foxes are starting to lose their winter coats.

May

So many people in this month believe wrongly that a litter of has been abandoned because no adults are observed with them. The reason is that the vixen chooses to lay away from the cubs. This I believe not only gives the vixen the opportunity to hunt for herself, but it will also wean the cubs off of her milk and on to solids. The vixen will visit the cubs regularly through the daylight hours either to regurgitate food for them or to bring them larger prey items. The earth and the surrounding area will be infested with flies feeding on the carcasses of food brought by the vixen for her cubs. If you do plan to watch in the vicinity of the earth be very quiet, for not only will the dog fox be lying close but you could deter the vixen from visiting her cubs, robbing them of a much needed meal. Be sure to put on insect repellant to combat the hundreds of flies and midges that will be attracted to this same area. Other watchers do not recommend this because of the scent of some of the lotions, but I feel that foxes rely so much more on movement than they do on scent, and if you do not have protection from these irritating insects you will be constantly swatting them.

Over the years I have found that about 10.00am the cubs are most active around the earth's mouth, but do not at this stage be tempted to place food around the earth.

It is in this month that poultry keepers and those who house pets such as rabbits outside report losses to the fox population. This is because the foxes, mainly the vixens, will be searching further afield for food for themselves and their cubs.

An increase in activity around the food site will provide you with hours of good observations. A lot of the time you will have already observed the adult foxes taking food away, presumably to cache. This month is no exception, although they may be returning to the cubs with it rather than cacheing it.

June

June is possibly the best month to observe cubs at play. They will use the same area regularly for playing and eating. Knowing where this area is will make things easier for the watcher and the photographer.

These play areas can usually be detected by the flattened grass caused by the rough and tumble games. Bird or rabbit remains may litter the area. The foxes' play area will also be visited regularly by the adult foxes who continue to bring food to the cubs, and even cubs this young can be observed cacheing surplus food. If you have yet to discover the whereabouts of the play area, usually the screaming of the fighting cubs will betray their presence to you. The breeding earth will be abandoned in this month possibly due to the heat and the smell, and the cubs, like the adults, will lie in hedgerows and ditches.

The cubs are always lying up close to each other and are still active during most of the day, yet become quite lethargic on hot days.

The cubs by this age are completely weaned off the vixen's milk, yet still rely on their parents for much of their food. The fighting cubs are not only sorting out a mini pecking order but they are also perfecting skills that will aid hunting. Possibly the mouse pounce is the most observed when cubs are fighting. Usually the fox cubs will direct this aggression on to the smallest of the litter, commonly known as 'the runt'.

July

The adults will now be bringing less food for the cubs, but will be taking them out on small excursions around known feeding areas. This is when the cubs are most likely to visit your food site. If the vixen detects you she will give out a bark-like call that will automatically send the cubs diving for cover. Do not attempt to take photographs of the cubs on their first visit to the food site. The most rewarding time I have found to watch adult and cubs foraging is about 9.30pm, and for morning watching from about 5.30am onwards. I have also found the foxes appear more relaxed in the early morning hours. The fox cubs will show some reluctance sometimes to follow the adults all the way up or down the field, and will sit down and play with one another noisily in the shadows.

I have found that in July for some reason the cubs are more likely to be split between foxes: two cubs with one adult, two with another. Whether or not this is a split between the sexes – male cubs with the dog fox, females with the vixen – remains to be seen. Do not feel that just because you observed only two fox cubs out of a litter of four with an adult that any others must have died.

Opportunities to take photographs present themselves during the day, for on hot days both adults and cubs will take advantage of the midday sun. Creeping around this area with camera ready can prove rewarding.

Towards the end of July you may find that it is only the cubs that come to feed on your offerings, usually announcing their approach by fighting and screaming, heard five minutes before you actually observe them. Now is a good time for photography as it probably won't bother them, and it is now you should be hoping to get some identification marks of the cubs. Do not mak e the mistake of naming the runt of the litter because it is the smallest and therefore easily recognized, because in a month or so the cub will have caught up in growth with the rest of its litter mates.

August

The cubs are usually the first to leave their day-time retreats, doing so usually about 8.00pm, in pairs. Once out and stretched, they will head off towards the play area, where they may seem to wait for the other litter mates to catch up before going on to forage, again usually in pairs. In the mornings the cubs are the last to bed down for the day and can often be observed hunting and fighting until about 9.00am.

In the latter half of the month, fox droppings can be seen to contain a high percentage of fruit such as blackberries and plum stones. This may explain why the cubs and adults may stop coming as regularly to your food site as before.

September

The fox cubs are now said to be indistinguishable from their parents, yet I believe a trained eye can still tell the difference. Tails are not as bushy as those of the adults, and the fox cubs, although feeding well, still look quite thin, giving the impression of a fox on stilts.

The cubs, now nearly fully grown, start to behave much like the adults in their times of emerging and departing.

Adults may start once again to feed at your food site although fruit is still high on the diet. The cubs, or I should say sub-adults, apparently choose to forage alone. Mornings provide excellent views of hunting foxes over land that has just been harvested.

After the last few months, however, at night at your food site observation can seem a little dull, for once again the fox's appearances become more sporadic.

Inter-family aggression is often heard. This is usually the sign of the fox family breaking up and some of the sub-adults may even disperse. September in the fox world it would appear means each fox for itself, and although you may still be lucky enough to observe two or three foxes feeding at your site, it will not last for ever.

Foxes are once again quite vocal. It may be that the sub-adults are either in the process of dispersing, attempting to keep in contact with the family whilst looking for a territory or that the resident foxes are becoming more hostile to their own offspring and warning them off.

The peak emergence time I have found for this time of year is about 7.00pm.

October

Although the adult foxes and some of the sub-adults may visit your food site, it seems like an afterthought, for they can be pinned down to no particular time. On warm wet nights, as is the case in most of the months of the year, foxes can be seen worming in the fields, sometimes as many as four or five in the same pasture.

Aggressive encounters, if not observed, can usually be heard and the calls of the foxes can be heard from 6.00pm onwards. Although a lot of aggression is observed in this month you may still see some play behaviour in the form of foxes chasing one another.

For the fox detective, field signs of foxes are beginning to accumulate around the borders and some around the earth used this year and in previous ones. Fox urine can often be detected along regular fox highways and entrances to fields. The increase in border marking suggests the dog fox may be redefining his territory in preparation of the breeding season.

November

More people see a fox for the first time in this month in their gardens, suggesting maybe that the break-up of the family group has led more foxes to disperse into new areas or that they are making short trips away from their regular areas. Many foxes are killed on our roads in this month suggesting they are moving into unknown areas.

Usually in one territory the vixen will have several earths on which she can fall back if needed, and all of these may now be showing signs of being investigated and excavated. In the latter half of this month the adult foxes visiting your food site may become more regular, and they usually start their night's foraging at 6.00pm.

December

With the mating season approaching, the foxes once again will be actively defending their territories. Calls from 5.30pm onwards will be very frequent, sometimes through to the early hours of the morning. Because of this increase in activity foxes can be observed in some areas throughout the day.

On some occasions in December after leaving food in my regular place, I have returned the next day after an unsuccessful watch only to discover the food still remains, possibly suggesting that much of the fox's time is spent around the borders of its territory.

Since the diet of a badger and a fox is pretty much the same, do not be surprised if you observe both animals feeding. The badger is the more dominant of the two.

—5—
Behaviour

Once you have got the hang of watching foxes successfully, then you may find yourself observing behaviour and unable to interpret it. There is a difference between instinctive and learnt behaviour. Much of what you observe in a fox cub's first weeks of life and onwards will also be observed in the adults; in this chapter I will describe what you see adults and cubs doing and show how, just by watching cubs, you will gain a great insight into the behaviour and postures of the adults; whilst successfully watching foxes is a pleasure, interpreting their interactions and being able to recognise these is the final piece of the fox watcher's jig-saw.

A good vixen mother will spend lots of time with her cubs, grooming them and generally keeping them clean. In the first few weeks she will lick their ano-genital area to stimulate the bowels, for the cubs without the vixen cannot urinate or defecate. Through this contact a bond will be formed. Instincts in the cubs will make them cry out if they are hungry or cold: usually a triple bark. They learn quickly that these calls will bring the vixen, the provider of food, security and warmth. The calls that were uttered through instinct, in later life, become calls of contact.

Fear

Another instinct observed when the cubs come above ground is the apparent fear yet curiosity of the unknown. The feeling of security for the young cubs must be in the fact that the earth smells of them and their mother; a fox in captivity when moved from its normal enclosure to a

Not only does grooming play an important part in bonding family members, it may be another way the fox family leaves its smell on each other. Many times you will see one fox just sliding its mouth down another fox's scruff, presumably leaving some sort of odour. Scientific explanations apart, the fox that is doing the grooming appears to like it as much as the fox being groomed. Grooming always seems to be done by a fox less dominant that the other, the exception being cubs.

new one will usually mark, both with urine and droppings straight away.

A cub finds out what must genuinely be feared by this method of cautious testing. It is said that a human baby will go through a stage of trusting everyone, yet another stage of suddenly fearing people unknown to them, this is called neophobia: a fear of the unknown. I believe that a fox cub will go through this neophobic stage when about twelve weeks of age. A fox cub in captivity will show little fear of strangers, giving one the impression they make excellent house pets. Yet at about three months, the cub, even with a lot of human contact, will suddenly show caution to strangers and run and climb the walls to get away; foxes do not make good pets, they are wild animals and this is where they belong! A fox cub, even though it may have been handled from an early age and kept as one would keep a puppy, will, despite this treatment and upbringing, still grow up to be a fox, with all the instincts and behaviour patterns of a wild fox. Worth bearing in mind is the fact that by keeping a fox cub as a pet you are condemning that animal to about fourteen long, lonely years behind bars; you would not get that sentence for murder!

You do hear of people feeding wild foxes out of their hands. This is something I have never felt the need to do, for two reasons. The first is simple: when you have a fox feeding out of your hand you have taken away the instinct of that fox to be wild, and the beauty of watching foxes lies in the knowledge you are watching a wild dog. The second reason is more for the fox: whilst the person feeding out of the hand may be doing so with all the best intentions, what happens when the fox, assuming all people are friendly and have food, approaches the next-door neighbour? I have been out on many occasions to rescue foxes that started off with fox-friendly people encouraging them to come close and then eventually feeding out of their hands, only for the people-friendly fox to walk straight up to children and get whacked with a golf club! Another stupid thing that people do is to make a fox cub lose its fear of dogs; next to man, dog is the fox's next enemy, a point worth bearing in mind when you want to introduce Bruno to Basil!

Both town and country foxes will have what is described as a 'flight distance': a distance that a wild fox will put between itself and you, in the knowledge that if you were to become hostile it would have enough space to get away. In the countryside the flight distance may be a couple of fields, whilst in an urban setting only ten or so feet, for the urban fox seems more able to live in a closer proximity with man; perhaps this is due to the fact that, although persecuted, urban foxes are persecuted to a lesser degree than rural ones. Whatever this flight distance may be, cutting it down due to interference by man is sure to be more of a disadvantage to the fox than an advantage.

Play

In the early part of a cub's life, as with many animals, play is a necessary learning tool. Partly it is to teach them to hunt, but also it shows where they stand in the pecking order and how to avoid attacks by their own family members. From the play area screams will often be heard, giving one the impression that the weakest cub is being killed. Don't worry, this is not so. Although the fights are becoming more frequent and

The play bow.

louder, most will not result in bloodshed. Body language is playing an important part in making sure of this.

When the cubs become older and a play area is selected, many items of play will be brought back for them. In the countryside, since moles seem distasteful to the adult foxes, they will usually bring them back for the cubs to play with. In many play areas I have found moles dead with teeth puncture marks, yet not eaten. Play items for urban fox cubs are a little more exciting and are often pinched from gardens, these can include: shoes, dog bones, balls and dishes, much to the annoyance of the householder when only one of their trainers can be found I must add!

A bag blowing in the wind will be enough to send them diving for the security of their underground refuge, yet minutes later they will be above ground again, approaching this very object. Eventually one of the cubs will investigate, yet still with extreme caution. It will approach the object almost on its belly. When the cub realises that the bag poses no threat it will be pounced on, mouthed and may even be eaten; the object may become something of a plaything for them all. The instigator is usually the bravest of the cubs, not necessarily the biggest. If none of the other cubs appear bothered by the new play item it may be paraded around near them to initiate play, and the play bow may be adopted.

Aggression

Whilst playing, the cubs are learning all the time and a mini pecking order will be established early; all the aggression is meted out on the weakest cub. I suppose if you are to start a fight, it helps if you know you will win, although I am sure the runt would not agree! Although the runt may be the weakest, it appears even this one can defend its share of the food, and when a portion of food is to be secured the cub will swing its backside around so the rear end is presented to the others (see illustration on p. 71, food defence). Along with this a loud clicking noise is made as a warning; even the bravest of cubs will only approach by sidling up and body slamming, rather than walking directly to it. Fox cubs in captivity appear to show little aggression to each other when eating cat or dog food, yet offer them something with fur or feather and the instinct to secure it will be observed, and heard!

Food

When outside the earth it is apparent that what can and cannot be eaten is learnt rather than instinctive, much like, I suppose, a human baby putting anything in its mouth. When the vixen or dog fox returns, the cubs will mob her or him, all rushing forwards, tails wagging, squealing with delight. They will possibly start nosing the corners of the adults' mouths in an attempt to get them to regurgitate food; if the adults have returned with a rabbit or bird this will be jumped upon and a fight to secure it will commence. When all the cubs' little round bellies are bloated usually sleep follows.

Cubs will often nose the corners of an adult's mouth in an attempt to get it to regurgitate food. This behaviour can also be observed in foxes greeting one another and also a submissive fox will greet a more dominant animal in this way.

Although there is enough food for both animals, the fox will attempt to discourage the hedgehog from eating by taking the food from underneath its nose.

Cacheing

Before this another instinct may be observed, this is the instinct of cacheing; I say instinct because the cubs don't necessarily know why they are doing it! Whilst many believe that the vixen teaches her cubs to cache, this is not so. A fox cub that has been found abandoned and brought in to be cared for, even when only days old, will in a few weeks' time start to try to cache. A cub in captivity will even attempt to cache in the lino of a kitchen floor; not that cubs in the wild are much better at cacheing initially, even their attempts will be haphazard.

Whilst I accept that a fox, rather than waste an abundance of food, will bury it, I feel it is not as straightforward as returning to the buried food supply when other food is short. When a fox visits a food site, it will carry off all the food possible. This seems to be the priority, before eating; when all the food has been cached the fox can be observed later on in the evening, retrieving it and eating it. From this behaviour I feel the fox is ensuring that it can secure as much of the food as possible before another fox or animal starts to eat, rather than purely hiding if for a future date.

I have often watched a fox coming and going from a food site, filling its mouth, going off to presumably bury the food, returning and repeating the actions. On many occasions when the fox has gone off to bury the food, a hedgehog starts to eat; when the fox returns, the fox will stay on site and attempt to eat from under the hedgehog's nose. Whilst this behaviour may seem selfish, in the wild it is the survival of the fittest, no different to the leopard of Africa dragging its kill up a tree.

When a fox does cache from a food site, does it cache the food that it likes best, or the food that it likes least? I have heard many people who feed foxes say that they know their particular foxes' preferences because it's the food that the fox will always eat on site. This can usually be disproved quite easily. If for example the visiting fox always eats the small cut-up pieces of bread on site, it could be said that this particular fox likes bread above all else. Yet if a loaf of bread was cut up into six pieces the fox will normally take this away. All the fox is doing it would appear is taking away the biggest and eating on site what would prove to be a waste of time and energy cacheing. Furthermore, to back up my theory, I have never observed a fox filling its mouth with raisins to take away to cache or for that matter earthworms! If a food preference study is to be undertaken I feel more accurate results would be gained if all the food was equal in size and weight. On the lighter side, I have also spoken to many people who rather than put food out on the ground have actually placed all the food in a carrier bag. This is done I am told to save the fox many journeys! (Any food preference tests here I assume would be 100% plastic!) This is not a good idea, as eating plastic can be dangerous for foxes. It is a mistake to assume that you should put out more food when there are cubs to feed; the number of foxes in a given area will increase with the amount of food available, so increasing the amount of food may lead to new foxes moving in.

Whilst the cacheing of food in the cubs is not something they appear to be that good at, adult foxes have the ability to cache just ten feet away from your observation point, and hide it so well that when you attempt to find it, it proves almost impossible. A well fed fox caches food very lazily, often leaving a wing of a bird sticking out of the ground. If the cache is a good one, from this we must conclude that other foxes are not meant to find it, and if this is so we must also assume a fox hunts for grubs and worms by hearing rather than scent; or else the food cached by a single fox would easily be found by the rest of the family. If this is right then the fox that makes the cache memorises its exact position. Biologists studying the cacheing behaviour of foxes have proved that the fox does remember the exact position of a cached supply of food and does not rely on its good nose to find it. They dug up a cache of food and re-buried it a few inches away from its original site; the fox returned to the spot where the cache had been, and did not smell the food that lay hidden only inches away.

A disturbed fox who may have been sleeping up for the day will run until a safe distance has been put between it and the disturber. It will then usually stop and turn around, I presume to check what the danger is. If no movement or noise comes from the area the fox will just amble off to the next cover; if the fox becomes aware of possible danger, it will bolt. The actions of a fox stopping and looking back have led to claims that when a fox is being chased by hounds, it obviously enjoys it because it will stop and wait for the hounds to catch up – a claim that I am sure only the hunters would make! If a fox were to continually run when the slightest danger presented itself, it would waste too much of its energy. The above claims are often backed up by saying that a fox can not be that disturbed by the chase, for when it has a safe distance between itself and the hounds it can sometimes be observed eating. Again when the fox feels the danger has passed it will continue with its normal life. One need only look to a warren of rabbits to observe the same behaviour; if a fox has just made a kill, the other rabbits, rather than bolting, will continue to graze. Prey animals can not live in constant fear of the predators for so much of their energy will be zapped if they were to do so.

What does it mean when a fox does this

Play-bow: This is when the cub, still standing, will go down on its front legs with its rear in the air.

Play posture: Having already described the posture of the play-bow, other body postures that initiate play are observed. The ears, although erect, take on more the likeness of wingnuts held at the side of the head rather than standing erect and the tail is held in its normal position. Pawing at another fox's back may also be observed in an attempt to get attention.

Submission: A cub that has lost against a litter mate will have its tail between its legs, its body arched; depending on how bad the beating was, it may be making a whiney noise. If the attack carries on, the cub may roll on its back and urinate with fear whilst a mixture of clicking and whining noises will be heard.

Surrender: Submissive behaviour is not the same as the behaviour observed in a fox surrendering. A submissive fox is not overly frightened of another higher ranking fox, it is merely showing good manners. The body will be held low, often dropping to the ground if the higher ranking fox approaches it. Cubs take on the submissive posture when the vixen or dog fox returns with food. They will rush towards the adult with tails wagging and start to nose the corners of the adults' mouths; these postures can be observed displayed from one cub to another.

Unsure: If a fox is uneasy, it will hold its ears back and continually rotate them and flick them from left to right. The fox will be trying to pick up any sounds from around the area and with its keen sense of smell will be sniffing for any give away smells. Whilst on the move, a fox unsure about a situation will approach an object or noise by semi circling and slowly getting in closer. If something to the fox is not right, it may just sit down and stare towards the area. A fox coming across a new food source, e.g. a food site, will usually show extreme caution, stretching its body towards the food, until the belly is almost on the ground. Any noise at this point will see the fox bolt for cover.

Dominance: A dominant cub will have its tail held high, its ears pricked. The dominant cub approaching a submissive cub will take on a stiff-legged walk; if an attack is launched, it will usually be direct with ears flattened to the side and tail still held high. On a slow approach to a submissive fox a dominant may also be observed to rub itself up against things like hedges and logs for example.

Pouncing: in play, a fox will often pounce into the air onto an object, something that when perfected will aid its hunting in the months to come.

When observed, the mouse pounce looks like a lot of effort for one vole or mouse. Why don't they just run up and catch it when it's detected? The answer is simple; to avoid being caught a mouse or vole will leap into the air, so the fox's action of coming from above rather than the side counteracts this.

Food defence: when a portion of food is to be secured the cub will swing its backside around so the rear end is presented to the others. Growls and clicking noises will also be heard and sometimes screams if the defender is the less dominant.

Equal status: two foxes that are equal in status will usually sidle up to one another, then body blocking and body slamming will usually start. Both will be showing a hint of fear and aggression; with bodies arched and plenty of clicking noises the foxes engage in what can only be described as a game of chess. If the body slamming continues and no one fox backs down then they may both go up onto their hind legs.

Fox trot: whilst this may look like a vulpine dance routine, it is actually the foxes' way of sorting out the pecking order without bloodshed. The winner, it would seem, is the one that manages to push the other off balance. Whilst both foxes' jaws will be open, usually neither receives a bite from the opponent.

Most of the noises and body postures that the cubs display can be observed in the adults, although most take on a far more serious role. Whilst the dominant fox will stand high, ears and tail erect, the submissive posture is the complete opposite. The cub-like approach by a submissive fox will normally be enough to prevent an outright attack. The submissive fox will go straight towards the dominant and lick at the sides of its mouth almost to give the dominant animal the impression of a cub, i.e. not to be attacked and of no threat. If this fails then the submissive adult will roll on its back exposing its genitals; sometimes it may even urinate whilst whimpering. The dominant fox will sniff the genitals and the outright attack is usually then avoided.

As in the cubs, body posture plays a very important part. The tail, ears and general body posture of a particular fox can be used to show both confidence and fear and also to initiate play. The tail, however, is not only used as a visual sign to other foxes, it can also be used to waft scents to other foxes.

About 8 centimetres (3 in) from the base of the tail is the violet gland; this can be clearly seen as a dark patch on the tail. With the lashing of tails in conflicts with other foxes, it no doubt conveys some message.

In all fox families there will be a hierarchy; the only family members who appear exempt from this are the cubs. Adults never display aggression to cubs – it would seem this is not socially acceptable. This could explain why submissive adults take on postures reminiscent of cubs, when approached by dominant foxes. They attempt to make their bodies as small as possible; they approach a dominant fox from this crouched posture and start to nose the corners of the mouth, again, from below. This cub-like behaviour exhibited to the more dominant foxes may also shed some light on how, through repression, the dominant vixen ensures none of the lower ranking vixens mate. Keeping the subordinate vixens cub-like in behaviour may also keep them cub-like in sexual maturity. It has been said that a dominant vixen will suppress the subordinate vixens from actually coming on heat, so this may be a clue as to how this is actually achieved. Also worth noting is that the subordinate vixens are always the more playful of the family group, and they, more than the dominant pair, will initiate play related behaviour (between adults).

As mentioned briefly, a fox that is kept in captivity and is introduced to another enclosure will mark it straight away, I reckon this is not so much a territorial marking, more a feeling of security. So within the territory, it could be that whilst the borders are marked against trespassing foxes, within the foxes home range it is done so more for that feeling of security within. One can only imagine how secure a fox must feel in an area that smells entirely of that fox or that fox family. For a trespassing fox, it would not only have the disadvantage of not knowing the area, but also being in an area that smells so much of the resident foxes. This could be why a trespassing fox is usually evicted from the land without a great deal of effort and why the landowning fox always appears to have the upper hand over the trespassing one.

Another behaviour observed in foxes, as mentioned earlier, is that on really windy nights the foxes are far more nervous. I suppose when one considers that a fox, rather than rely on sight as much as it does its sense of smell and hearing will on a windy night not be able to rely on them much as much as normal. When hunting, though, wind can be a blessing as well as a curse: the problems they have with smelling and hearing will also be experienced by their prey. Ground-nesting birds will rather take the gamble against a fox and stay in their nests on a really windy night than take to the air. The opposite is true of rabbits; on windy nights they move further away from their burrows.

Mating

Since there are only three days in the mating season in which the vixen is receptive, she must ensure that at the right time there is a dog fox around to mate with. And the dog fox must ensure that when the vixen is ready to mate he is there to oblige. In the days leading up to mating both the vixen and the dog fox throw caution to the wind; it seems apparent they have only got one thing on their minds, and their safety takes second place, so it is not uncommon to see both of them during the day apparently unperturbed by what is going on around them.

The vixen, when nearing this date, has a tendency to wander further than normal; she will also be urinating often. Although she is not ready to mate, the dog fox, through the urine, can tell that she is coming into season. His part is to trail the vixen until she is ready. Many times during this trailing the dog fox will attempt to mount the vixen and if she is not ready he will be attacked; it appears it is the vixen who is the more dominant of the two in this season. On some occasions the vixen, rather than attack the dog fox, will just either swirl around to prevent him mounting her, or she will sit down. Whilst the dog fox's attentions may appear at times too much for the vixen to tolerate, this pre-mating or courtship ensures he will be available when required.

When the vixen does urinate the dog fox will show great interest in her urine and at times may even be observed licking it up or at the very least marking over the top of it. I have had many reports of vixens being trailed by two or three dog foxes in this season, though regrettably I have never observed this myself. I feel maybe the dog foxes could be itinerant foxes, that is to say they have no territory and they are all trying for the attention of the vixen.

Something that may be observed during this courtship period is the dog fox pawing at the vixen's back. If she is ready she will not move and he will mount. What usually happens is that when the critical time for the vixen has arrived she will prance around the dog fox with her tail held high and then much sniffing around the genitals by both foxes will commence. When the ritualised sniffing is over the dog fox will move behind the vixen, and the vixen will hold her tail to the left or right, this I presume is to allow the dog fox to gain easy access. The dog fox will grasp the vixen with his front two legs and start to mate.

It is said that the dog fox is not completely erect until he has actually entered the vixen, then his penis become completely erect and the base of it starts to swell. In addition, the vixen's vagina will constrict, this is what causes both animals to be locked together; commonly called the 'tie'. After the dog fox ejaculates he attempts to dismount and since they are still locked together he brings one of his back legs over the vixen's back and there they stand for the duration of the tie.

When the pair finally unlock, the dog fox usually licks at his genitals, suggesting maybe the tie is a painful experience. The vixen however shows no signs of discomfort before or after the event and can often be observed frolicking around almost in celebration.

Since there are litters of cubs born as early as December and January, I assume these are the litters of older vixens (i.e. those over one

Commonly called 'the tie', this is probably as painful as it looks, but it is nature's way of ensuring that the dog fox delivers sperm successfully.

year old)who come into heat earlier, and this would explain also why dog foxes are fertile between December and February, to ensure that when there is a mature vixen ready to mate there will be a fertile dog fox. Since the peak cubbing time is March probably most vixens giving birth are young vixens rather than older ones; this further supports the evidence that unfortunately foxes do not live very long in the wild.

Even before the vixen becomes pregnant, several instincts will become evident. She will start to dig an earth; in an urban area this maybe under a garden shed, whilst in the countryside she will excavate rabbit burrows or use disused badger tunnels. Instinct, not past experience, will tell her to select two or three good sites as a fall back. Instinct will tell her to build the earth on a bank or slope, ensuring if there was a downpour her newborn cubs would not drown. This behaviour cannot be put down to experience since even yearling vixens will go through the same processes.

A dog fox through instinct will bring food to the vixen and drop it at the mouth of the earth, before and after she has given birth. Quite remarkable since foxes are, to say the least, very selfish with their food.

A fox's instinct tells it must eat, and its learnt behaviour ensures that it does just that.Unlike man who appears to live to eat, most other animals, whether predator or prey, eat to live. Many of the questions as to why a fox does a certain thing may always remain unanswered. We must remember that the fox evolved millions of years ago; no doubt much of their instincts and some of their behaviour may be somewhat irrelevant in today's world. The fox now has no natural predators, yet then the wolf roamed the countryside along with other predators. The landscape and fauna were different; no doubt some of the prey animals about then are now extinct.

The cacheing of food may have been to secure it from other scavengers, rather than the idea today that the fox stores a surplus supply. Eating food only to regurgitate it later today seems an oddity, yet then it was probably safer to take food back in the belly rather than the mouth, discouraging therefore the unwanted attentions of any other scavengers or would be predators.

At times a fox may act in a way totally out of character with its species and we should not assume that there will always be a scientific explanation. Like people, foxes too have their different personalities and unusual quirks!

This photograph and the one on the front cover are of two cubs belonging to a family of foxes, a family affectionately known as the 'Whispa' family. The photographer Adam Chennells encouraged the foxes to the site where he planned to photograph them by using Cadbury Whispa bars!

—6—
Research

How much research you do depends on how much free time you have. On many occasions the fox receives a bad press whether it be about overbreeding or causing damage to householders. Researching these aspects through questionnaires and by observation may shed light on the areas of conflict. Giving newspapers facts and figures, rather than mere opinions, certainly adds more weight to the defence of the foxes. If a questionnaire reveals that the majority of residents are fox-friendly, local papers will normally pick up the story. Any good press for the fox has to be seen as a positive step forward. In this chapter I hope to give you some ideas which you could put into practice, furthering your knowledge of not only the fox family you are studying but also different fox families around your county.

Analysing fox droppings

To some, the idea of pulling apart a fox's dropping to discover what the foxes are eating at certain times of the year is in itself off-putting, but to the fox detective who would like to know as much as possible about the foxes being watched this is a must. You will gain an insight into the fox's main food source throughout the year, and being aware of exactly what they are eating will help you understand where they may be feeding. You do not have to have hundreds of pounds' worth of specialist equipment, and you certainly do not have to be a scientist to attempt this form of diet study.

All you need to analyse fox droppings are a low powered micro-scope 100 x 200 x 300, a pipette, a couple of dishes, a fine sieve, forceps and possibly a few storage jars and labels. You will also need some small bags; freezer bags are ideal.

If you have followed the guidelines as laid out in previous chapters, finding your fox droppings should not pose a problem. On finding them, collect them into a bag, securely tie and label it with the date and area they were discovered. Once you have collected possibly four or five, the night before you plan to analyse them, leave them in your storage jars in water to soak. This makes them a lot easier to pull apart the next day. They will by the next day have started to break up, and using your forceps you can easily separate the rest.

The first thing to determine is whether the dropping contains the remains of earthworms. Using your pipette, get a small drop full of the sediment from inside the jar and place it on a microscope slide. If the dropping contains the remains of earthworms you will see several needle-like yellow/orange objects. These are the tiny bristles that are found in the worm's skin, and the correct term for them is 'chaetae'.

Place the rest of the droppings into the sieve and wash them, preferably under running water, maybe an outside tap. Soon all that will remain in the sieve will be the components of the fox's diet: pieces of bone, feather, insect remains. Separate all the different components; all the feathers in one dish, the bones in another and so on. This will then give you some indication as to the amount of each food source taken. Attempting, for instance, to determine what bird a certain feather came from, or what mammal a certain bone or hair came from can start to get a little more difficult, and although there are books available to help, keep your study as simple as possible at first. Assuming you have started analysing droppings in January, get a sheet of paper, mark the top 'January' and note the contents of your findings under a heading of 'Week One'. Starting with the most abundant find in the dropping, score each on a scale of one to six, see box on next page.

In this case, feathers and bird remains were the most abundant, so

week one	one	feathers and bird remains.
	two	mammal hair and bones.
	three	grass and other vegetation.
	four	earthworm remains.
	five	scavenged items.
	six	other

they have gone in to the box marked 'One'. Scavenged items can be discovered if there are plenty of bones within the dropping without any fur or feather, and sometimes items like tin foil will also be discovered.

Mark your following week, 'Week Two' and follow the same steps. Once you have completed a month's analysis you could either draw a pie graph or a normal graph. The idea of the monthly graph is to work out the most important food source throughout by totalling the occurrence of items in your weekly boxes. By doing this over the months you will discover just what the foxes eat in each month of the year, and what items are the most important. The more droppings you analyse from your area the more accurate your findings will be.

The acid in the fox's stomach is such that all that would remain of a vole would possibly be the jawbones and a little of the vole's hair. The abundance of grass I have discovered in fox droppings I believe is due specifically to the acid mentioned above and I have found when there is an abundance of grass there is little else other than earthworm chaetae. This suggests that the fox maybe eating the grass to counteract the build up of stomach acids.

The most important aspect to bear in mind is to always sterilise all equipment used and be as hygiene conscious as possible.

If you have also marked down on your paper/notebook the areas from which you collected the droppings through the months, a pattern should appear which may give some indicate the size of the foxes' territory. You could also start to place small coloured pieces of wool inside the food you provide for the foxes. You may then discover these when analysing the droppings, giving you some idea on the distances some of your feeding foxes travel.

Questionnaires

When foxwatching you can be in one place only at one time. Assuming you have managed to encourage the fox or foxes to feed at your food site, how can you determine how many foxes are in the family group? How can you discover if your food site is just one of many visited throughout the foxes' night-time excursions? How can you discover if some foxes of the same family you are studying are feeding at the same time, yet somewhere else? The simple and most effective answer I have found is to compile a householder questionnaire. You do not need to get hundreds printed; you could just start with the houses that either look on to your area or back on to it. Once you have been to these houses with a questionnaire you could select another ten and so on.

Too many questions on your sheet will put many people off answering any of them. The best solution is to keep the number of questions down to a maximum of eight.

Most of the questions you will be asking will assume that foxes do visit the garden, so be sure to ask questions that will prove useful to your watching and research. I have done an example on the next page to give you some idea of how to lay out your questions and what sort of questions to ask. Please note, however, that it is just an example and questions will vary according to the area you are studying. You will gain the householder's trust if you include your name, address and phone number. This in itself tells the people that you can be contacted, so your intentions cannot be bad.

A short introduction giving the reasons why you would like answers

Questionnaire to householders

your name
your address
your post code
your telephone number
date

I am presently studying the foxes in this area and as part of my study I am attempting to determine how many people have foxes visit their gardens, and how many people actually encourage foxes into their gardens to feed them. I have compiled a short list of questions that would help my study no end so would appreciate it if you could find the time to answer them. At the bottom of the questionnaire is the date I will be returning to collect the form. If you have any questions on my study, please do not hesitate to contact me.................thank you.

NAME . . . .

ADDRESS . . . .

1. Do foxes visit your garden ?Yes ❏   No ❏   if yes, how many ? . . . . .

2. Do you feed the foxes ? Yes ❏   No ❏   if yes, on what? . . . .

. . . .

3. What time do the foxes visit ? . . . .

4. Have you taken any photographs of the foxes which I could see?

. . . .

5. Have you noticed any distinguishing marks on the visiting foxes?

. . . .

6. Do the adults bring cubs to your garden? Yes ❏   No ❏

7. Have you lost any livestock to foxes? Yes ❏   No ❏   if yes, please state.

. . . .

8. Are foxes causing you a nuisance? Yes ❏   No ❏   if yes, please state

. . . .

Thank you for the time it has taken to fill out this questionnaire, I can assure you that all information will be strictly confidential. I will call back for the completed form on . . . . (date)

to the questions posed gives the householder an idea of your study. By leaving a date when you will collect the questionnaire will, in most cases, ensure it will not be thrown away.

Try to ask questions that will need only a yes or no answer, or at the very least just a line of writing. Most people will be put off if the questionnaire involves writing an essay.

Depending on your chosen study area you could also compile a questionnaire aimed specifically at farmers and landowners. You could then discover why farmers dislike the fox, how much per annum does the fox cost the farmer from predation of livestock, and if the farmer allows fox-hunting on his land. If you gain the trust of the particular farmer or landowner ask if you could watch the foxes from his land, and if he knows of the whereabouts of the foxes' breeding earth; and, if so, whether he would disclose this information.

Most farmers however are a little suspect to say the least about any-one with an interest in foxes so be warned, I have on many occasions been told where to stick my questionnaire!

Analysing fox teeth

While out taking part in a field study, you may often find fox skulls or jawbones. It is possible to age a fox skull if the jawbone is still near by, for it is the teeth that are used when working out the age of the partic-ular fox when it died.

On the many occasions when I have discovered fox's skulls and jaw-bones they have always been in ditches, hedgerows, by side of the road or near excavated badger setts or fox's earths. You may also discover the skulls of badgers. The simple way to tell the difference between the two is that badger skulls will mostly have the jawbones still attached, whereas the fox's skulls do not. If you do discover a fox's skull always look around the vicinity for the jawbones.

Most of the skulls you find will need cleaning, some more than others depending on how long the bones have been there. The most effective way of cleaning the skulls and jawbones is by immersing them in a bucket of water with a high concentration of bleach. Leave the bones to soak for about three days, clean off any excess dirt with an old nail brush. On a sunny day leave the bones out to dry. Once clean and dry, label the skull with the date and location where it was found. Also label the jawbones.

The size of the skull may give some indication of the age. Young foxes' skulls will not have developed the long snout of the adult. Another indication could be the wear on the teeth. The less wear, the younger the fox. This method however is not foolproof because it really depends on what the foxes are eating. If yours have been eating rice pudding, their teeth will be nice and sharp.

The most effective and reliable way of ageing a fox's teeth is to analyse them under a microscope once they are prepared. In this preparation I would suggest you enrol the help of a science teacher from your local school. Although it is possible to do the experiment yourself, your local school will have all the facilities needed and, by enrolling their help, you may be able to get a project going for the pupils to undertake.

The same method of ageing trees applies to the ageing of teeth. When a cross section of a tree is cut you can count the rings and gain an insight into its age. It is exactly the same for foxes' teeth.

In each year of a fox's life it develops a ring in the cementum of its teeth. Soaking one of the teeth in a weak solution of nitric acid for about three days will cause the calcium to be removed. The tooth will then be soft enough to cut with a scalpel blade. Thin sections should be cut; place the section in dye, and then the annual rings can be counted using a microscope. The more teeth that you can analyse from different jawbones you discover in your area, the more you can plot with some degree of accuracy the mortality rate of the foxes in the vicinity.

Casts of foxes' tracks

Foxes' footprints should be easily found. After a few days the tracks will become less distinct and will eventually disappear, but you can record them by making plaster casts. The items you need can be carried in a your pocket. If you find a good print, you can take a cast straight away. You will need some strips of card about 12 inches (30 centimetres) long and 2 inches (5 centimetres) wide, some paper clips to form a circle with the card, some plaster of paris, a bowl in which to mix the plaster, a spoon to mix it with and some small bags to put the mould in when still damp. You could take water with you, or if water is nearby just take a container to collect it in.

Do not just choose any track. Look around until you have found the clearest one. On selecting your track make a circle with your card and paper clips to completely cover the print without disturbing it. Push the card circle into the ground around the track and then mix your plaster of paris until it is quite stiff, ensuring you use enough to cover the track. Once your mixture is ready it should be poured into the circle to a depth of about 1 inch (2½ centimetres) and left for about twenty minutes. It should then have gone hard but not completely dry. Ease out the whole circle with the cast gently with the help of your spoon. Include any of the mud below it. Place your cast in your plastic bag; when home it can be taken out of the cardboard circle and carefully cleaned up after a couple of hours.

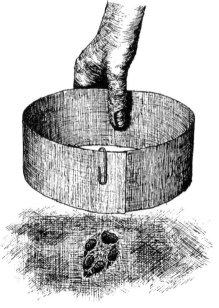

Once it is completely dry you can either leave it as it is or alternatively paint or varnish it. If you plan to do a lot of these casts it may be worth noting the date and location on the underneath.

Know your area and who's there

I cannot stress enough the importance of knowing your area almost as intimately as the animals that live in it. Do not have a blinkered approach to any animal other than foxes. If, for example, you find a vole tunnel or a nest containing field mice these may answer some questions about a fox in this area. Learning to interpret the signs of animals other than foxes can be a help to the serious fox watcher; learning the habits of the animals that foxes predate would also be useful. Knowing the warning signs can increase your chances of watching the hunting fox.

Carrying a small field guide around with you may help you identify plants, trees and mammals. You really cannot have too much information in your diary notes. You should also be fully aware of the rules of the countryside: respect all wildlife and fauna and do nothing to endanger or destroy any part of it.

Once you have become quite adept at foxwatching, always, before going out, decide on what question you would most like answered. It may be what are the foxes doing when they arrive in a certain field or what is it that attracts the foxes to this field? Whatever the question, it should become your goal to find the correct answer. Without questioning your observations, you will learn nothing other than that the foxes are visiting your food site to eat.

If a fox is often observed walking up one particular hedge line it may be because behind the hedge there is a rabbit warren. The fox may also be patrolling and marking the borders of its territory. By asking yourself the question and taking it upon yourself to find the answer you may observe a fox stalking a rabbit or even watch a territorial dispute between the neighbouring foxes. Through your questions you will be learning all the time and observing different interactions which would have otherwise been missed.

—7—
Fox Friends

Foxes are so poorly understood, so badly treated and unfortunately so inadequately represented, that many people who have a passion for foxes feel isolated. The same applies to those who feed foxes. It is something they very rarely shout about.

By forming a group, not only will you bring together a number of people interested in foxes and their welfare, you will also be giving something back to the foxes. A group of dedicated people can make all the difference, not just from the aspect of research, but also by helping to dispel the many misconceptions associated with our friend the fox. By forming a group you can help the fox by improving people's understanding. As a group you can have your say on how badly you feel the fox is treated and most importantly you and your members will be the voice of the fox, the fox's advocate.

The first step in your attempt to get a group up and running is to gain people's interest first, so a name should be selected upon early. By having a name you will have the identity needed for publicity purposes. Then you should decide on what exactly you would like the group to set out to do. There would be no response if every time you had a phone call from a person interested in joining, you could not tell them of the group's aims. As a guideline why not model your group on another wildlife group in your area, for example the badger group?

Many people who have not had the pleasure of watching foxes in the wild might be tempted into joining your group if you were to take them out to your area to watch your foxes. You do not need to be an expert on foxes to form a group, and with the watching and research you have done to date, you will know more than most on the subject.

How can you expect anyone who has never been out foxwatching, who has never observed a fox, to be passionate about them and be impelled into doing something positive for their welfare? It is usually when the fox is observed that most people realise that they are not the size of a wolf, that they are not the cat killers as often thought, but that they are beautiful animals which should be allowed to live free from the persecution they presently receive.

Foxwatching can be educative. If for example the fox arrives at your food site, and takes food away in its mouth to cache, you can tell your guests this is what happens when a fox has come across an abundance of food. Rather than waste it, it takes advantage and buries it for a day when food may be in short supply.

Even if you never hear again from the people you have taken out foxwatching, you can be sure when they hear people depicting the fox as a bloodthirsty, cunning animal, they will correct the misconception.

The National Fox Welfare Society (see useful addresses) is encouraging support groups around the country and will give all the advice needed in forming and running a group.

I hope to give you some ideas that can be put easily into practice, thus not only furthering your research but also proving beneficial to the foxes.

Until now, you have watched foxes in your study area, you have studied the land the foxes live and breed on, but because your observations are of one family only, you cannot base your conclusions and theories on this. By forming a group and helping members to find their own areas within your county, you will have access to studies and observations of several other fox families.

If each member or watcher sent you their observations each month, a larger picture, and therefore a larger study area would be formed. For example, in your area over, say, a three-year period, the foxes you are studying may have had four cubs in each of those years, but to say the average litter size in your county is four would be wrong unless you had enough data to back up your claim. Although you would be correct to say that the foxes you are studying have an average litter size of four, other fox families in the area might average three or five. To gain a fair sample, you would need data from over fifteen fox families; obviously, the more the better.

Assuming also that each member chose to analyse the fox droppings in their area, in the way described in the earlier chapter, this information, when pooled, would give your research more credibility. You could, with ease and accuracy, plot the foxes' diet for the county, discovering the most important food source for each month of the year. Remember research is your most important tool for successful watching. If you then give talks to groups, it would be far better to say it is a fact that the most important food for the foxes in this county is..., rather than saying 'I think '.

If over a period of time you had collected a hundred questionnaires from your study area, and these showed that of the hundred people questioned, 20% feed the same foxes as yourself and 50% like the foxes visiting their gardens and only 30% see the fox as vermin and actively discourage it from their gardens, this for your personal study would be invaluable, but would not be accurate enough on a larger scale. If your members did the same in their areas, and all the data was again pooled, you might then be faced with research that would interest your local county paper. Ask: did you know in this county, out of the five thousand people who filled out a questionnaire only 10% would actively discourage the fox from their gardens and 35% actively encourage them? Any good press the fox receives through accurate research can only be seen as a positive step in bringing about a more enlightened public with a more fox-friendly attitude. Within your group you could now see from the questionnaires who felt the fox is a pest because of the damage it causes in certain gardens, because of the loss of pets such as rabbits. You could call upon these people and ask if they would like advice on a particular fox problem they are having.

How do I stop the foxes digging up my garden?

You do not have to be an expert. Believe me, many of the complaints people have against foxes are easily solved; for example, foxes very rarely dig up householder's gardens for the sake of it. It may be that a fox is just concentrating in one spot much to the annoyance of the householder. Just asking a few simple questions can sometimes not only reveal the reasons for the fox's behaviour but can also provide a solution to the problem. Many keen gardeners will use bonemeal on their gardens and a fox smelling this on top of the soil and below the roots of plants will assume that there is a cached supply of food, and start to dig. On finding nothing edible the fox will just leave the plants uprooted. The simple solution is to advise the gardener to stop using the bonemeal!

How can I deter them from digging under my garden shed?

Another common complaint in the early part of the year is of foxes building earths under garden sheds and summer houses. Although some people would gain from this great pleasure, we must appreciate that not all will view the fox with the same passion as our own. So what can be done? Usually the householder will have already attempted to block the hole with large stones, and will have found that rather than discouraging the fox they have actually increased the problem, mainly because the vixen will dig a larger hole around the obstruction. Some householders are just pleased to hear that the foxes will not be living under the shed for the rest of their lives, for after a very short time the vixen and the cubs will abandon their underground refuge. Some people will be willing to wait until the foxes have abandoned the shed area before ensuring it is properly blocked, to prevent the same happening the following year.

Others however will not be as obliging. They will want the foxes out sooner rather than later. Can anything be done? I would most certainly not even consider cage trapping the foxes, for two reasons: removing foxes and their cubs will be not only prove distressing for them, but also create a problem of where would you put them. You cannot just take them to a field and release them. This is against the law, and should be against your principles anyway, because the foxes would certainly not survive.

The second reason is that because foxes are territorial the moment a territory becomes vacant, another fox family will move in, so not only is cage trapping distressing for the foxes it is also ineffective in solving any problems.

The only reliable way of deterring foxes without harming them is by using an approved animal chemical deterrent, for example, Renardine 72-2. The instructions for use are on the back of the tin and there is a National Fox Welfare Society advice line listed at the back of this book that would be willing to tell you where your nearest supplier is and advise on its use. They also offer advice on foxes injured or orphaned. Chemical deterrents can be used to deter foxes from leaving their droppings on people's lawns and deter them from digging. At this point it is worth noting that some people may advise to use diesel oil or creosote as a form of deterrent against foxes, but using any chemical to deter foxes which is not approved as an animal deterrent would in fact be breaking the law and would leave you open to prosecution. In addition I do not think it can be that effective anyway, considering that in most urban areas people creosote their fences, yet the foxes still remain!

Most people's problems with foxes either come from ignorance of the facts, an unwillingness to face the facts, or come from ingrained attitudes deriving from the stories about the crafty, cunning fox that are always told to us at a young impressionable age. Most problems can be solved just by telling people the facts about foxes; for example that there is no proof that a fox will attack and kill a full grown cat.

Just having an insight into the fox's seasonal activities throughout the year will give you some understanding as to why the fox is doing something. Always bear this in mind before jumping in feet first to solve a problem that would, three weeks down the line, have solved itself.

How to stop them eating pets

There is no denying that foxes will kill pet guinea pigs and rabbits if the opportunity arises. The fox will always look for an easy meal, so how can people guard against predation of their pets by the fox? It is unfortunate that most people do not realise that they have foxes visiting their gardens until they lose their rabbit to one.

The message is clear: prevention is far better than cure. People keeping pets outside should ensure that the hutches are foxproof. Weld mesh is better than chicken wire because foxes will chew through chicken wire with ease. Another important aspect is that the catch on the door should not be the sort that can be pulled down or pushed up. It must be a secure one that can only be opened by man and not fox. It is a common mistake even by the householders who realise that foxes are in the area to assume that foxes hunt only at night, so they make the mistake of giving their rabbit a free run of the garden during the day.

Because most people realise they have foxes only when the fox kills their pet, it may be useful for your group to issue a press release to your county papers telling people that even if they do not believe that foxes visit their gardens, they should always ensure their pets are properly housed and protected. This is the prevention; there is no cure if you are called out and the rabbit is already dead.

I include the following story of a fox and a chicken shed to give you some idea of a fox problem which had a householder distraught because of a loss of chickens nightly and to show how easy the solution was, not only protecting the chickens but also offering an alternative to the pest control officers being called in.

I was called out to a lady who was losing her chickens at night to the fox. On entering her land I counted six chicken sheds, yet only one was receiving the attention of the fox, and it was only from this one that the fox was stealing the chickens. I found all but the problem shed were off the ground, so the foxes could not dig their way in. The problem shed however was just on the soil, so all the fox had to do was dig a small tunnel, which it had successfully done, and it would be in amongst the chickens. When this was pointed out to the lady in question she said that although she could see what I was saying was right, it would cost far too much money to raise the shed off the ground and to fit a floor. The simple, and the cheaper solution I suggested was to put paving slabs down on the inside of the shed, so even if the fox was to dig under, it would never come up within the shed; problem solved. Usually all that is required is a little common sense, without even a knowledge of the fox . If you ever do go out to a problem, and you are not sure how to advise on the solution, do not make the mistake of bluffing. You and your group will lose all credibility, and put the fox at undue risk. You would be respected more if you said, 'I am not sure, but can I try this?' or, 'I will get back to you after discussing this specific problem with someone more experienced.'

Another form of research you could undertake in your area that would prove not only interesting to you, but beneficial to the fox, is monitoring road traffic accidents involving foxes. If every member of your group contacted you when they observed a fox dead on the side of the road, this would provide you with details about how many foxes died on the roads; whether more males than females died in particular months of the year; and plotting where they are dying may give you an indication also of where they are living. How does counting dead fox bodies on the side of the roads prove beneficial to the fox? If all your members are told that not only do you want an accurate map location of the dead fox but you also want details on the sex and approximate age, then most members will have to get out of the car for a closer inspection, thus helping the fox.

Many foxes when hit by a car may not be fatally injured. Some may have concussion or a few broken bones. Because a fox is lying still on the side of the road many people assume that it is dead, and without a doubt, if it's not dead it soon will be, for the chances are it will get hit by a car again. If you and your members approach these foxes on the side of the road, you may discover that a fox originally thought dead is still breathing. Care must be taken to ensure that removal of the animal off the side of the road is done correctly, not just for the fox's sake, but also for your own protection. A brilliant book that tells you what to do in these cases is the one by Les Stocker entitled *The Complete Fox*.

Just through simple research like monitoring road deaths, not only can you glean a wealth of information, you may also be able to do something positive and save a fox's life. If you went out to a thousand foxes and only one of these proved to be still alive and you saved its life, then it would have all been worthwhile. When you talk to people about foxes, or you take them out to foxwatch, if out of a thousand you just manage to change the views of few then you are succeeding. In most of your group's activities you may find that you do not need to fundraise often, because most of what you are all putting in is time, and this costs nothing. If you feel you would like to help organisations locally, organisations that help injured, orphaned and sick foxes so making useful contacts if ever an emergency did arise, then this is possible without a great deal of effort.

Many wild animal rescue centres or wildlife hospitals are self-funded, or at the least under-funded, but they still have to feed the animals brought in for care and attention, which still have to be given medication. So how can you and your group help? One of the easiest ways is to collect about six large cardboard boxes, decorate them with illustrations, photographs and drawings of foxes. Stick a card on the front of the box asking members of the public to donate a tin of dog food for the rescue centre, wildlife hospital of your choice. Distribute these boxes in pet shops and supermarkets. Once they are full, take all the tins and donate them to the organization of your choice. Sometimes shop keepers will allow you to display a box in their shops indefinitely, so providing a regular supply of free food to the centres in the most need of it.

Alternatively you could also arrange a boot-sale or jumble sale, the proceeds of which can be donated. Through these actions not only will you be doing something constructive for the fox and for the centre of your choice, you will, by being out there, gain more members, more recognition and ultimately more support.

Forming a group turns into a two-way deal for you and the fox; you meet people with interests within the same field as your own, you broaden your research, therefore broadening your knowledge, you gain the satisfaction that you are helping the animal that you most admire. The fox, through your efforts, will receive a little more protection and help, will be understood more by a larger number of people, and, through you and your group, will gain a voice. You obviously cannot help every fox in the country, but doing what you can certainly makes a difference.

Further Reading

Anon, *The Facts About Fox Hunting* (RSPCA, 1988)

Anon, *The red fox – friend or foe?* (From League Against Cruel Sports,1993)

Ashby, E., *The Secret Life of The New Forest* (Chatto & Windus, London,1989)

Bang, P., & P. Dahlstrom (Collins, London,1990) *Collins Guide To Animal Tracks and Signs.*

Burrows, R., *Wild Fox* (David & Charles, Devon, 1968)

Fitzgerald, B. Vesey, *Town Fox, Country Fox* (Deutsch, London, 1965)

Ginsberg, J.R., & D. Macdonald, *Foxes, Wolves, Jackals, and Dogs* (IUCN,1990)

Harris, S., *Urban Foxes* (Whittet Books, London,1986)

Harris, S., & D. Macdonald, *Orphaned Foxes* (RSPCA,1988)

Hewson, R.,*Victim of Myth* (League Against Cruel Sports, 1990)

Kolb, H., *Country Foxes* (Whittet Books, London, 1996)

Lloyd, H. G.,*The Red Fox* (B. T. Batsford, London, 1980)

Macdonald, D., *Running With The Fox* (Unwin Hyman, London, 1987)

Macdonald, D., & P. Doncaster, *Foxes in Your Neighbourhood?* (RSPCA, 1982)

Stocker, L., *The Complete Fox* (Chatto & Windus, London, 1994)

Strachan, Rob, *Mammal Detective* (Whittet Books, London, 1995)

Useful Addresses

Care For The Wild, 1 Ashfold, Horsham Road, Rusper, West Sussex RH12 4QX

The Fox Project, Old Chapel, Bradford Street, Tonbridge, Kent TN9 1AW

Helios Homeopathic Pharmacy, 97 Camden Rd, Tunbridge Wells, Kent TN1 2QR Phone 01892 537254/536393 Fax 01892 546850

Hunt Saboteurs Association, PO Box 2786, Brighton BN2 2AX

League Against Cruel Sports, Sparling House, 83-87 Union Street, London SE1 1SG

Mammal Society, 15 Cloisters Business Centre, 8 Battersea Park Rd, London SW8 4BG

National Fox Welfare Society, 32 Bradfield Close, Rushden, Northants, NN10 OEP. Tel/Fax 01933 411996

People's Trust for Endangered Species, 15 Cloisters House, 8 Battersea Park Road, London SW8 4BG

Royal Society for the Prevention of Cruelty to Animals, Wildlife Unit, Causeway, Horsham, West Sussex RH12 1HG

Scottish Society for the Prevention of Cruelty to Animals, 19 Melville Street, Edinburgh EH3 7PL

Wildlife Hospitals

C.A.R.E.S. Wildlife Hospital, 58 Station Road, Haddenham, Cambs.

Hydestile Wildlife Hospital, New Road, Hydestile, Godalming, Surrey

Secret World, Badger & Wildlife Rescue Centre, East Huntspill, Nr Highbridge, Somerset TA9 3PZ

Wildlife Hospital Trust, Aston Road, Haddenham, Aylesbury, Bucks HP17 8AF